UNDERSTANDING THAT MATTERS

Arguments and Opinions

Gina P. Viray-Raley

ISBN 978-1-0790-1697-0

Images from Pixabay

Printed in the United States of America

I dedicated this book to my late father who was looking forward to seeing me graduated my higher education. Unfortunately, he passed away before it happened. Although he is gone, I am certain that he is happy now that I have finished and fulfilled his wish. I love you, Tatay

UNDERSTANDING THAT MATTERS

Arguments and Opinions

CONTENTS

PREFACE

Understanding That Matters: Arguments and Opinions is a compilation of original and graded written compositions on various topics in business management. You will learn in this book an understanding and insights that I discussed in each subject. At the same time, you can also create your own ideas about each of the subject matters. This could serve as a learning process as you read this book particularly if you have interest in dealing or managing with business in the United States as it is based on American system. However, educating yourself in business is almost the same principle in United States as in the other side of the world. You may neither agree nor disagree with the arguments and opinions I made in these essays. Nevertheless, it is significant that I have to share my thoughts and ideas with you. Hence, I am hoping that you will have the pleasure of reading my book. Enjoy!

INTRODUCTION

Writing an essay is not an easy thing to do. You should have patients and wisdom when you are finding your arguments on every subject matter that you are about to discuss. This was my personal experience when I was writing these essays which will require inspiration and time in accomplishing the task. But before I go further, let me ask you of what is an essay? According to my own understanding, an essay is a composition expressing your ideas and thoughts on a certain topic of discussion. I guess that you would find the definition of an essay similar with any other sources. It is true that writing an essay is not an easy task. In my case, I placed all initiative and interests to research all related topics that I explained in all of my essays.

One of the most important points that you have to remember when writing an essay is, it should be free from plagiarism. In other words, it should be a unique piece of composition. You are not allowed to copy and paste the work of another person. Moreover, it is necessary that you use proper grammar. Usually, it won't allow you or better not to use perfect tenses in your statements. However, it is sometimes difficult to avoid usage of this tense on each sentence but I believe that it is also accepted and proper as long that these correspond to the statement. I always stood in my belief in these essays which gave me a positive result from my grades. At least, I had a chance to practice my writing abilities in a

3

most challenging way which would be an advantage for career opportunities.

The essays that I have written in this book are forty-eight compositions which I completed on about 4 and ½ years. Each course is divided into four essays on related topics in business management. It took me long to complete these essays because I have a full time job of current employment. For this reason, I could only do it during my free or available times. In these essays, I expressed my understanding and ideas in different subjects and questions on each subjects. In each composition, I have learned various approaches to reach the conclusion of the arguments with a reasonable way of thinking. This book would remind me the hard work I placed in each and every essay that I have written. Nonetheless, I really enjoyed doing it since I have a keen interest in research writing especially the topics involved were about business that I have enthusiasm for. Likewise, the essays included in this book will give you a better comprehension and knowledge regarding specific topic of interest.

ESSAY TOPICS

HUMAN RESOURCE MANAGEMENT

Distinguished between the Vietnam Era Veteran's Readjustment Act (VEVRA) and the Uniformed Services Employment and Reemployment Act (USERA).

The Vietnam Era Veterans Readjustment Act (VEVRA) and Uniformed Services Employment and Reemployment *Rights* Act (USERA) are only two of employment legislation acts that are included by most of the companies and firms in their employment rules and regulations. These two acts are strict laws and passed to secure veterans from discrimination and to give equal protection rights Although, both of these laws enforced the same by Department of Labor of Veterans Employment and Training Service (VETS), they are different in some areas. In order to identify these differences, I would consider information on the following questions regarding these two laws:

1. Who are covered or protected?
2. What is the goal or aim?
3. What are the requirements for eligibility?
4. Where to file a complaint?

The VEVRA applies to all Vietnam era veterans, special disabled veterans, or those who served during a war event or an expedition with a permitted campaign badge. This act was first enacted in 1972 and as amended in 1974. With VEVRA as amended (*38 U.S.C. 4212*), federal contractors and subcontractors of $25,000 or more are obliged to take affirmative action to hire those who are qualified and eligible individuals under this act. This means that the covered employers have an obligation to list and provide all vacancy positions with the exceptions of all executive and top management jobs, positions that will fill up by internal recruitment, and jobs that only last less than three days with the local state employment development service.

In the event of Gulf War in early 1990's, I have learned that they were some serious observations, remarks and concerns occurred when the employees returned to their civilian jobs from their military service during the war. For this reason, a law was passed and signed in 1994 to provide the rights and remedies of protected employees, known as USERA. In contrast with VEVRA, this act is to assure that after any individual returned from military duty or have served in the uniformed services whether voluntary or involuntarily will have the right to return to their previous or current jobs or re-apply for employment for a successive period of time of absence not exceeding five years except for some jobs that are with limited time of employment, such as summer or short contractual jobs. According to the law, duration of time absence from work not exceeding five years have with some exemption to the rule such as periodic service or training, call duty for national emergency or other related events. USERA protects most of veterans, whether their service is in Air Force, National Guard or Army, and whose absence from their civilian employment is due to military obligation or training. Unlike with VEVRA, affirmative action is not a requirement for covered employers.

In the case of violations and refusal on the part of employers, they are quite different on how and where you file the complaint. As stated in the codes under Department of Labor, two agencies are involved in handling its complaint. In USERA, the VETS is the agency authorized to conduct a close examination and make a resolution on the complaint. However, if the result or outcome of the resolution is not successful, the complaint can be send to the Department of Justice for consideration and forward it before the judge in the proper District Court. With VEVRA, if any federal contractor or subcontractor failed or decline to follow the provision of this act, the complaint can be file with the Department of Labor's Office of Federal Contract Compliance Programs (OFCCP) who perform an investigation and take applicable proceedings under the codes and regulations of the law.

During the course of my study in this subject, I noticed that with VEVRA, veterans who use this act are the ones who served in the war in the past like in Vietnam War years and those who were discharged with disabilities. And with USERA, it is used by many veterans who serve on any military duty whether in the past, present, or future. But regardless of their differences, it is advantageous and encouraging to any citizens of the United States who is and was a veteran. Lastly, being a veteran can be enjoyable and fulfilling while, the same time enjoy the rights of American soldiers in accordance with the regulations between VEVRA and USERA.

---

1 *Lepak, David, Human Resource Management, 1ˢᵗ Ed. New Jersey: Pearson, 2009.*
2 *Department of Labor, Equal Employment Opportunity/Compliance, www.dol.gov.*

Examine the advantages to hiring internally to fill vacancies within an organization.

Internal Recruitment is a method for recruiting process in hiring employees to fill a vacant position within the company. Recruiting process is relatively long and costly for any company, especially for large corporation. For this reason, many choose to hire internal applicant for any vacancy that may arise to gain benefits in term of expenses and time savings. Here are the lists of the advantages that I would like to illustrate further as follows:

1. The cost is less and quicker.
2. It can retain committed employees.
3. The training period will be shorter.
4. It will have good lists of candidates.

The big advantage of internal recruitment is the cost and how company can minimize the expenses for advertising. Next question is how these employees will know about the position. Job posting is one way to reach the internal applicants. Also, companies usually have staff meetings, putting up in notice boards or in their newsletter to reach internal applicants. In my experience when I was working in International Labor Organization, they were passing a memorandum about the vacancy announcement. If they were interested in applying for the job, they were invited to file an application. At that time, Internet was not widely used yet. ILO have official website but we did not have Intranet back then, which is now a company's private access for employees and members of the organization. A company who has Human Resource Department can make it quicker and faster to inform the applicants who are to be called for a test. Internal Recruitment usually eliminates the initial interview and proceeds to the test based on the position available. This was what happened when I was transferred to another department in I.L.O. Mostly, the one who is on the top prospective employee to be hired has the chance to be approach first and offer the job. In this case, the manager can save time and effort to speak and communicate well and quicker with the prospective employee. If he/she accepted the offer, then it will be a huge benefit in terms of cost and time filling up that position. Usually internal candidate is not asking for a bigger salary. On the other hand, the salary is normally increased with a reasonable raise when an employee landed a new position.

Either big or small company, each manager who shows appreciation and value of the services of their worker is very important. So there is a reason for them to show their loyalty and commitment to the company. Most of the times, they treat their workplace as their home and co workers as their family. If you are truly committed and motivated to be productive in your work, there is always a chance for future advancement. The fact that you know already the organizational culture, values and system of the company, you are feel confident to meet the needs of the company.

It is important that whenever a new position has been filled up, the question comes up if the newly hired have enough skills, knowledge, and abilities about the job. As an employee, you are not just learning and getting use on your job but also gaining knowledge about the culture and values of the company from day to day operation. For example when I began working in my present job, I have learned to do multi tasks in different divisions. When one of my colleagues quit the job, I was offered the position and replaced her training program called continuing education which is related on the job at the circuit court. In this way, we can learn new and updated system on the legal field. It can save a lot of time on the part of employer or either employee that will lead to a shorter period of time for training somebody for transfer or hiring internally. Certainly, it will reduce the cost of training as well.

Nowadays, companies have a searchable database of employees in which it should be maintained to be updated at all times. This tool is designed to make easier for the company to select who are the lists qualified for the job and it will help to size down the number of candidates. This is an important process and huge advantage for large corporations like Coca Cola or Pepsi. The fact that the manager is the best person who knows about their worker's performances, it will be also very useful if he has a periodic evaluation among all the employees to determine who best workers are.

For all these advantages illustrated, I would say that the internal recruitment helps to improve and create a better bond between employee and employer relationship. Moreover, this is an excellent method to move the employees around within the organization and to have a lesser stress creating a new job design for any new position.

Lepak, David, Human Resource Management, 1ˢᵗ Ed. New Jersey: Pearson, 2009.

Identify and describe three programs related to OSHA and employers obligation to follow or participate in them.

Occupational Safety and Health Act known as OSHA is another law signed and passed in 1971 to secure that all employees are safe and free from any harm or risk of accident in their workplace. Just like any other law or act, employers have the obligation to comply with the standard rules and regulations under OSHA. They are three programs related to this act. These are: inspection program, workplace violence program, and ergonomics.

There is a system for inspection priority under OSHA. In this program, an inspection will be enforced for any report of risk or danger in any workplace. If there are accidents or any casualties about five or more resulted while at work, OSHA will provide an investigation. Lastly, is respond to any complaints by an employee who believed that the working condition is not healthy or safe. This means that an employee has the right to report any kind of violations under this act and can request inspection with or without consent of their employer. The employee has the right to know what the outcome of the inspection is. On the other hand, employers have the responsibility to cooperate and provide any necessary measures to perform this inspection. In addition, industries considered having a high hazard environment such as waste and recycle, construction, or any related manufacturing companies are required to have a programmed routine inspection. For most cases, this is done traditionally to avoid the danger of possible chemical exposure or reasonable certainty of danger that might occur. For double security and safety, OSHA administers a follow up examination and assures that the workplace is free from any danger or accident.

The second program is workplace violence program. This program is very essential and not only important on the actual risk of any violence that concerns by the employees against co workers but also from outside of the workplace, especially when dealing with the public. But what are these violences or serious concerns that this program is protected. Some examples are when one of co worker threat or harass the other co worker, somebody from outside try to rob the workplace, or if dealing with customer service and started to have confrontation that leads to a fight. The place where I am working at present is a good example for any disturbances or danger of violence that might exist. For example, it was one day after the court hearing due to desperation of the defendant that he was lost the custody for his child over the other party; he went crazy in the parking lot. Right then, he was arrested since Sheriff Office is in our building too. This is the reason that we are not advice to stay outside after work if we have to wait for our ride, especially when everybody left the building already. Aside from having sheriff department in our workplace, we have also installed security devices such as camera, alarm in every offices, hallways, and around the building, and check-in security at the door. It will be avoided any thing will happen or might happen either arising from a customer service or somebody who is trying to make trouble inside the office or even outside the building. Workplace like we have, an employer should provide an extra safety measures for the sake of the employees as well as the public. For other security measures like good lightning in the location, proper direction of exit or barrier between employee and customer will help to reduce any violence in a workplace.

As also discussed in Chapter 4, ergonomics is the third program. But how this program works in any workplace? It will help employees at work to relieve stress and provide right positions while doing the job. This is effective to address any musculoskeletal disorders (MSDs) in the workplace. When I was younger and worked in this company, the air conditioner was near beside me and was blowing directly on my back. As a result, I got a severe back pain that caused me to have called muscular contraction. If any workplace is like this, it may affect the productivity of any work and could also lead to work related sickness. Every company should have a proper design of the workplace with a healthy working station. Comfortable chairs, proper height of any computers, or proper heat and air installation can help the job done more efficient without any harm and enjoyable while working too. Employers have the obligation to furnish their workers a stress free working environment and provide them a training that will illustrate them on how ergonomics works to improve the well-being of the employees. Managers have the duty to review whenever circumstances occurred related to any musculoskeletal disorders and accidents related. These records should be accurate and submit appropriate report to OSHA.

As an employee, it is the right to have a safe and healthful workplace and employers have the responsibility on how to keep their workers to be safe while at work. It is important that employers should ensure their employees to have a safety and health training program in order to avoid any kind of injuries, accident or danger of violence that may occur. For this reason, any employee will feel secure, happy, and safe while on the job. At the same time, they can be more productive and motivated to work in a positive way. Moreover, if any employers comply with this law; they will take advantage on the costs of any compensation claims due to accident or injuries.

Lepak, David, <u>Human Resource Management</u>, 1ˢᵗ Ed. New Jersey: Pearson, 2009.

What is unfair labor practice (ULP)? Identify the 5 ULP's identified by the Wagner Act.

An unfair labor practices (ULP's) is refer to any practice or action that reject or deny the statutes under National Labor Relation Act (NLRA) also known as Wagner Act in which this is another body of law to protect employees from their employer or any labor union organization in exercising their rights. According to the law, they are five ULP's that defines and involves under this act. These are as follows:

1. To interfere with, restrain or coerce employees in exercising their rights.
2. To dominate or interfere with the formation or administration of labor organization.
3. Discrimination against workers regarding hiring, term, or any kind of condition of employment either to encourage or discourage joining the union.
4. To discharge or discriminate against worker for filing charges and providing testimony under the law.
5. Rejecting to bargain collectively with employee's chosen representative.

Under Section 7 of NLRA, it covers numerous basic rights where employees can benefit against their employers and any labor organization. In this manner, they cannot interfere or restrain them in exercising these rights. There are various examples to illustrate employee's benefits of this act. For example, an employer is trying to get information from their employees about union activity and request them to report about what are their plans in the future. Sometimes employer threatens their workers that they may jeopardize their job if they are part of that activity by laying off, firing or terminating them. This law guarantees them the right not to answer any inquiry that the employer is trying to obtain about the union. You have the right to reject and not participate in taking part of the employer's tactics to get employer in trouble for not accommodating them on such inquiry.

It is your right under this act that you have the freedom to join or form an organization. What does it refers to? For example, a labor union tries to force you to join on their organization or ask you to pay some kind of monetary contribution or donation to support it. As a general rule stated in the law, employees have the right to join labor union whenever they want to. They can choose who they think who can give them the best representation on their behalf. Any union may not able to force or exert pressure on you to engage as a member. On the other hand, employees are still covered on this rule even if you are not a member of any union. For example, if two or more workers or an employee is speaking on behalf of a group of workers to take an action to their employer to address some concern about work related issues such as safety concern, working condition or even improving pay salary. This is just as the same right to have or join a strike in representation under labor union.

Certainly, any companies or organization do not want their workers to join in any kind of unions. It is illegal for them to treat similar action on their employees differently when it comes to a union membership. This is what happened if the employers know their employees is a member of a union and circulating some sort of petition, signed a union authorization card, or maybe encouraging co workers to join a union. They will either discharge or demote their employee whoever involved in that union activity. Some employers transfer or assign them in more difficult work or task. On the other hand, it is also illegal to enforce or make hiring agreements as a condition of employment. Most of the times, the one which are more qualified are the ones refuse for employment due to their security agreements. In this case, it violates the rights of an employee because as stated any employer can not treat their workers differently for being a member and not a member of a union. Such action may result to discouragement to join a union due to fear of possible mistreatment by the employer.

The fourth line of the section covers to those who filed a complaint or give any information or statement as a witness to certain case, and or testifies in arbitration. As a result of this action, the employer punishes an employee by transferring to an undesirable work as a disciplinary action. The employer cannot implement this behavior as a punishment or being part in any NLRB proceedings because you are protected under this act.

The last ULP stated in the first page is about bargaining. In this section, an employer and a chosen union representative by the employee have the duty to bargain in good faith on resolving an issue. This means that both sides will give an active participation with a fair and open mind to reach a desirable agreement. Employer's failure to negotiate or settle an issue under these circumstances will result to unfair labor practice.

As an employee, it is a privilege to exercise rights under NLRA where it can give firm guidelines either on the part of employers or union organization to prevent from committing any illegal action. In this case, an employee can be assured that he/ she will be treated with respect and not to be deprived of life and liberty. Otherwise, any prohibition will be resulted to unfair labor practice which can be reported to NLRB who performs an investigation and applicable proceedings in this matter. Finally, compliance of this law and cooperation either on the part of employer or union will improve a better management and labor relation within an organization.

1Lepak, David, *Human Resource Management*, 1ˢᵗ ed. New Jersey: Pearson, 2009.
2National Relation Labor Board, *Employee Rights*, http://www.nlrb.gov/rights-we-protect/employee-rights.
3National Relation Labor Board, *NLRA*, www.nlrb.gov/national-labor-relations-act.

INTERNATIONAL BUSINESS
MANAGEMENT

NAFTA has left all three nations, U.S., Mexico and Canada "better off than they would have been without it." Do you agree with this statement? Evaluate the success of NAFTA ten years after it became effective.

North American Free Trade Agreement (NAFTA) came into effect in 1994 and signed by United States, Canada, and Mexico which can create more jobs, increase trade, expand economy, and improve the standard of living and other environmental protection. As NAFTA's main goal is to free trade from barriers between the three nations, it covers broader issues in consideration to disagree or agree if they would have been better off without it. Let us examine the effect of NAFTA among the three countries.

First, let us take the case in United States. Bonnie Long said, "We're the losers" because lots of American lost jobs due to manufacturing relocation in Mexico and Canada. In this scenario, the winners are the big corporations who can move and relocate their factories abroad, especially in Mexico where they can get the cheapest wages and materials. For example, Wal-Mart is one of the biggest retail stores where most of their products are manufactured abroad and brings greater profit and wealth to its owners and stockholders. Small companies like locally owned manufacturer, Gerald Trolz could not benefit in this opportunity because he could not afford to relocate his business so he remain in operation in Indiana. For this reason, the outcome of outsourcing is the rising unemployment rate where American lost jobs massively in manufacturing especially in places like Midwest. There are also losses in production of goods in which these products should have been manufactured and made in U.S.A. Consequently, this is why America has more imports than exports that led to an increasing trade deficit with Canada and Mexico. This problem might not be entirely caused by NAFTA because part of these job losses is because of globalization. But according to Gary Hufbauer, a senior analyst at the Institute for International Economics said that "NAFTA is the symbol of that pain." The other argument on NAFTA is the increasing arrival of illegal immigrants from Mexico which has becoming deeper. I would not think that NAFTA has a direct responsibility on this matter. However, I believe that it also contributes conflict on the issue. Let me stress more the Mexico in relation with this matter.

Among the three nations, Mexico is considered as the weakest member of the free trade agreement. It is true that NAFTA created more jobs in Mexico by expanding trade-driven assembly lines known as maquiladoras in which U.S. owned companies hired Mexican workers on the side of the border for cheaper labor and wages. Unfortunately, the life of Mexicans under this program has been exploited and the condition got worse that led to deterioration of Mexican environment. NAFTA seemed to fail maintaining the human needs and well-being of the Mexican people such as fair wages, working condition, housing, hospitals and schools. As a result, many of these maquiladoras program has been vanished and eliminated. This could be the reason why many Mexicans force to cross to the border searching for a better life while it is an increasing illegal immigration in the U.S. At this point, Mexico would have been better off with NAFTA since that there is no firm progress has given them. Instead, more of their citizens have moved north to the border to look for jobs. The expectation of Mexico that their economic difficulties might be resolved through NAFTA was just an imagination where their government effort to make their country a more competitive and more realistic in life has been ignored and left behind because of it.

On the other hand, Canada seems to be the one that benefits most in NAFTA. Perhaps, it is for the reason that they have a more open mind about free trade agreement. It is something either, "you eat and you live or if you don't, you die"; it is a win or win situation. It only shows their faith on NAFTA will work for their citizens and their government especially that they have more well educated people to benefit for better jobs such as skilled workers in manufacturing business. Though they have some pain endured according to their Prime Minister Jean Chretien, progress has proven in NAFTA by shaping them with a greater competitive economy.

NAFTA might have some shortcomings and challenges but after a decade it has shown success too. As the world largest free trade, it was certainly achieved its purpose. The exports and foreign investment opportunities has been significantly resulted in overall growth. According to US Trade Representative, Robert Zoellick, America has doubled its trade especially the agricultural export to Mexico and Canada. Mexico has driven to civilize and build up their economy, culture and system of government. Foremost, it has increasing growth of global competition among the three nations especially Canada which is now far more export-oriented in the marketplace after NAFTA. They even created more jobs and more than doubled its export to the U.S. Also, other several sectors like gas and oil services are increasingly fast. In spite of success stories, it could not weigh the struggles that U.S.A and Mexico has brought by NAFTA.

In conclusion, NAFTA have both negative and positive impact among the three nations. I certainly believed that NAFTA did not bring U.S. and Mexico to prosperity. In fact, the reality that U.S. loses the strength of its industrial capabilities becomes negative effect in the economy and to the American citizens. Even its supporters thought that the agreement of free trade is not enough to benefit all especially between U.S. and Mexico which is close to have economic gap. In addition, the growing of illegal immigration is related to the matter that Mexican exporting more people rather than products in the U.S. has gotten worst after NAFTA. Even if, the mentality of Canada of adapting agreement rather than arguing about it, I still believe that Canada would have been better without it.

At present, it continues to debate about the future of the free trade agreement. Unless, NAFTA will take some steps or pass some reforms for the issues created due to this agreement, it will create more lack of balance in many circumstances which can cause more bad economic condition among other countries in the future,

Deresky, <u>International Management: Managing Across Borders and Cultures,</u> 5[h] ed., New Jersey: Pearson, 2006.

In what ways might the American style of negotiation be misinterpreted in another culture?

One of the most substantial accomplishments in international management is the ability to negotiate effectively with other countries. The cross-cultural negotiations with different nationalities is not easy because it may create great difficulties and misunderstanding due to cultural differences, language, process of decision making, value system, or any non verbal behaviors and attitudes inherent in a given culture which are part of the overall process of negotiation. These factors are ways that can cause a problem in international business negotiations. The following paragraphs will demonstrate how American style of negotiations misinterpreted in another culture.

There are stages in process of negotiations. One of the most significant stages for most part in the world is to build relationship. How this will work in the negotiation style of American? We know that American is famous with punctuality since they value their time. During negotiations, they do not want to waste any time in getting down to the business. If the foreign business negotiator would like to take enough time to build trust and respect as a primary element of negotiation, it will be destruction on Americans because their style of their negotiation will be interfered. Some of business negotiator like Middle Easterners would like to get acquainted on their first meeting which means that they will have general discussion and concession before going to an actual business. This stage in the negotiation has always been hard to the American because they are the most impatient person in the world. So how a foreign negotiator could misinterpret their action on this matter? They would think that Americans are neglectful in building up relationship with them or avoiding the process of precise negotiation.

American aspect in exchanging task related information or session of presentation and other discussion is being a straightforward and objective to the subject. They talk straight and direct to the point and do not like to interrupt. They are not like French who loves to debate and Chinese who often ask questions in negotiation. When I was working in International Labor Organization, I was working with different nationalities that have distinct cultures. I have observed some cultural differences in those meetings that we had, American in particular. It is certainly true that they are good in talking but not as a listener. In general, this action often misinterprets American for being not committed or attentive in the discussion and lack of interest for what others have to say. In addition, they also misinterpret the tone of American to have arrogance and superiority in their voice. Perhaps, Americans are confident that their knowledge of the information presented to their counterpart or within the group is comprehensible on a logical basis.

The fact that the value of time for American is very important part of their agenda, this is also way to misinterpret by other foreigners in the negotiation. Because they want to do the business right away, this could be mistaken as a rough tactics to their counterpart as to pressure them into making a decision quickly. For instance, Russian has a different behavior when it comes to time value since that they are always late in any meeting and likes to stall. They do not comply as to what Americans thinks that "time is money". Just like other negotiator, Russians are more patient and determined. Further, this subject is again related in building up relationship with the foreign negotiators especially Asian who are accustomed to a long detailed negotiation. You cannot rush up your business with them since this is their cornerstone in business agreement.

Among all other foreign business negotiator, Japanese is often the one that American have negotiations. They are skillful negotiator who takes a lot of effort of studying and bringing their counterpart own cultural background and its business practice. In contrast with American which has less background with regard to other culture, Japanese thinks that they are not concern with their culture and only interested to get the business at once. Japanese and American does not seem to have the same in common in many of their standards. Japanese have more strict rules about their culture related areas in business that American must comply. If you do not know about your counterpart, it will likely to create a lot of misunderstanding. For example, American talks straight to the point like 'yes or no", if Japanese heard you say "no" during negotiation, they would misinterpret it as to not agreeing or not optimistic about the information or proposal that they are presenting. For this reason, they will avoid smiling where smile is their sign of being friendly or simply choose to leave the room rather than giving negative response. I know this could be frustrating to Americans since they are frank and direct where this action can also be misinterpreted as rudeness and shows as a lack of discipline for other culture. Instead of saying any negative word, it is better to explain or suggest another statement where you do not actually mean 'no' as we are not able do the deal.

In the last stage of negotiation, American takes contract seriously. But for other foreign business negotiator, this is considered as an insult or waste of money especially Asian who prefer to do their agreement based on trust and comprehension of the proposal. For other non verbal communication, American could misinterpret their physical gestures and body language into different meaning such as having an eye contact while speaking. This gesture considers as anything resembles arrogance and disrespectful on African or Asian counterpart.

In business negotiation, it is very essential to learn about your counterpart's cultural background because different culture and behavior have different view in different subject. Moreover, cross-cultural misinterpretations can all have negative consequences in business negotiation. In order to avoid misunderstanding, American should adjust their negotiation style and technique that they can understand the culture and approaches to business on their counterpart. If you have knowledge of cultural differences on your counterpart, it will allow them to understand your behavior and the process of the negotiation to make it easier and smooth.

Deresky, <u>International Management: Managing Across Borders and Cultures,</u> 5ʰ ed., New Jersey: Pearson, 2006.

Discuss four guidelines that could be followed to increase the likelihood of success for alliances.

In today's business world, strategic alliance is been used by many companies who wants to expand and grow more the business. It is commonly use in international business management which involves an arrangement in business between two or more companies who combine their effort to pursue various purpose and mutual benefit while achieving new opportunity. In alliance, it may benefit the firm to establish a large-scale of competencies, technologies or expand into foreign market over a competitor efficiently. However, the company should give careful consideration on forming an alliance not only on the success segment but also problems that might encounter in its creation. In order to reduce the possible risks and to increase the possibility of success for alliances, they are four guidelines that should be followed. These are: choose a partner with compatible strategic goals and objectives; seek alliance where complimentary skills, product and markets will result; work out with the partner how proprietary technology or competitively sensitive information will be handled; and recognize that most alliances last only a few years and will probably break up once a partner feels that it has incorporated the skills and information it needs to go it alone.

Selecting a partner is the first most important thing to consider in alliance. The prospective partner should have compatible goal and resources in the management style with their company. It might not be exactly the same but at least they will complement and understand each other company's vision, strengths or limitations and capabilities. For example, Thomson who is selling electronics combined their business with TCL, a maker of T.V. sets with their same objective to be top on multimedia electronics in the marketplace. At this point, it is a very critical time for company management to recognize and comprehend on how to select an effective partner especially when it is a cross-border partnership where cultural incompatibility is always the problem. So to make sure that you are choosing a right partner, you must analyze what you are searching for a partner and make list of questions to ask before executing an arrangement in alliance. If your selection is success, it will lead to the association of right partner providing to accomplish the business a common goal which will bring both of the partners a greater level of success and to grow more in the future.

Secondly, it is vital in alliance that the partners acknowledge their skills and technologies to be shared to ensure a better outcome of the business. This means that each partner must be in accord to bring their special and unique skills into the alliance either technical or knowledge in the market. If for some reasons that one partner is good in the area of technology and the other is in market research, it will be helpful to perform and to cover up in that area where the partner lacking the capability. To have a balance relationship, the partners must develop a new skill and strategies within the alliance which is beneficial for the success and growth of the business.

The third guideline is with regards on the information and technology to be shared with your selected partner in alliance. This means that you do not have to give all company information to your partner but just the right ones that will be use to grow the business. Partners should have the level of trust, commitment and adequate confidence to their partner so that it will allow them to work well together. With trust, partners can share their ideas with an open mind and can make an agreeable decision making that will increase the productivity and efficiency of the partnership. This is the reason that it requires the company's managers to build interpersonal relationship in which helps to build trust and create a friendly relations between individuals while working in a desirable way. Trust is a very importance factor in alliance. Without it, the partnership in this agreement will likely dissolve in the early formation of alliance. However, the alliance should be supported by a formal agreement where various issues in relation with the creation of the alliance should be addressed and settled.

When forming an alliance, it is best to identify and discuss the strategic, managerial matters, expectation in organizational issues, and other relevant subjects that take place during the strategic alliance process. In this time, the managers and employees have the opportunity to educate efficiently with the new intangible skill and capabilities from the new partner that will be adapted the knowledge into its own partnership and learn how to handle problems in the future. By setting your strategy with your partner, it will develop a better operational plan of the business which benefit from the relationship of both partners. For instance, there was a major argument between the partners in alliance of KLM Royal Dutch Airlines and Northwest Airlines on how to run the business whether in European or American way. The problem in the cross-border alliance is often difficult to collaborate effectively due to some issues like cultural difference in which they have distinct history in their management or economic system and ways of practice in business. In such a case, it is necessary that the partners in alliance should operate the business with their combined skills, a new developed technology and equal contribution of strategies in their partnership. So when partners are working together as one company, the result will be flexible and mutual in which it will accomplish favorably than doing it alone like saying "two heads is better than one".

Alliance is like a marriage where a long courtship will be in process to assure that the prospective partner is the right one. This is the same concept when you are entering an alliance. The company needs to evaluate competence, capital and the vision of the partners and reassure that your product and services are aligned with the other company. If the guidelines are properly followed, the partnership will certainly be successful and will bring a strong competitive advantage to new market and knowledge in the new approach in technology.

Deresky, <u>International Management: Managing Across Borders and Cultures,</u> 5^h ed., New Jersey: Pearson, 2006.

Discuss the role of "reverse culture shock" in the repatriation process. What can companies do to avoid this problem?

One of the most challenging parts of the human resource management of a company is to have an effective and successful repatriation process from international job assignment of a manager as a continuing course of a job. The fact that some firms are not really mindful about the effect of reverse culture shock that will be faced by a repatriate, the outcome of repatriation is always different from each person or family because they have different experiences in which the adjustment takes place in their own timing and aspect in life. However, it is important for the management to have reentry phase of career cycle where manager's experience from working abroad can be acknowledge and useful in a company. In the next paragraphs, I will discuss further about the role of reverse culture shock in the repatriation process and how it can be avoided by a company.

Many repatriates do not think that they need any form of repatriation training or counseling after finishing their contract abroad. Why would they? It is their home country where they know their own culture and ways of life. For instance, I never had any kind of program to prepare me of the expectations on my home country when I went home on the first time. Unfortunately, going back home can be more frustrating and tough than moving for foreign job assignment especially after a period of time working abroad. Actually, I had reverse culture shock the first time I went home where I was confused and felt lost. It was even harder to deal it than the culture shock that I had in the early years in Switzerland.

Some companies do not have programs that repatriates may need because of the training costs or absence of proficiency in the program. As a matter of fact, it did not even reach 50% of those who had a formal training in repatriation based on the survey made by American Society of Personnel Administration International (ASPAI). Repatriation program is not only an advantage to a repatriate and family but it is an opportunity for the managers to maintain their knowledge about intercultural relations. I know that some American sees a foreign assignment as a negative move but I believed that it can be certainly rewarding and an enormous career advantage as well personality development upon returning to a home country. This is the case in any United Nation's office if they send any employee on international assignment within a certain period of time; he or she will be promoted upon returning to the home office in Switzerland.

Even so, the problem in working from foreign assignment is when the time to move or go back to the home country. This is particularly true when you are away for a very long time since that you are already accustomed with the culture of the foreign country where you were assigned or worked. It is hard to get back to your old ways which make you depress or stress because of not getting back to the flow of your personal life as well in your working place. You will realize that once you arrived in your home country, things have changed in numerous social and general aspects. The once you called there's no place like home will seem foreign at your own country now. This was exactly what I felt the first time that I came home. The only thing that did not change is my relationship with my family because we have close family ties and we frequently continue to communicate. Nevertheless, I was lost contact with other relatives and people that I knew before and I felt lack of interest to reach them out.

As a repatriate, it will be a more tough time when you return back to your home office. The fact that most repatriates obtained new and great skills from their work abroad; they may find it boring on their present job. Some of them will be disoriented and feel alienated in the workplace. Not just your work is your concern but the adjustment of normal standard of living will certainly change too. It will be a more serious effect if the repatriation process will be with your family considering that your spouse's career was been kept on hold while she or he was abroad. Moreover, it is important for the children to feel welcome in their new school environment.

So what a company can do to prevent reverse culture shock from their work or other personal issues related to the matter? In order to ease the adjustment process of repatriation, the company should increase the long-term use of their global cadre. This means that the company considers managing a proper arrangement for repatriation while still overseas. In order to be connected, it is vital that there will be a frequent communication between the home office and the expatriate about work-related information. In this case, the expatriate will feel that he is still part of the organization. It is also helpful if the new skills, knowledge and experience developed by the repatriate while abroad can be applied and recognized in the home company. Further, the repatriates should have to raise issue what are their concerns so the company may decide the right kind of benefits that they may need as not all company offer this kind of opportunity. According to research, there are some other support systems that can help the repatriation process to be effective and successful such as mentoring. This is an opportunity of the expatriate to discuss with his or her mentor on any concerns both work-related or personal issues and changes or development within the home office. As an alternative, there is also called special organizational group with the same purpose as in mentoring program.

In conclusion, repatriation is very important process for the repatriate to ease the reverse culture shock that may occur. It is essential for every company to support the repatriate and the family by providing a well developed repatriation programs to ensure that they can quickly and successfully adjusted to the home country. This smooth repatriation process will not only benefit a repatriate but importantly a company itself who value their employee.

Deresky, International Management: Managing Across Borders and Cultures, 5ʰ ed., New Jersey: Pearson, 2006.

FINANCIAL MANAGEMENT

What is the goal of the firm and, therefore, of all managers and employees? Discuss how one measures achievement and the key decision variables of this goal? Do you agree with this goal? Why and why not?

Some businessman may imply that main goal of the financial management is to earn the maximum profit; this should not be the objective of the firm. In the world of business, a company must consider all factors and aspects in making financial decisions, such as gaining higher market share, cash flows available to the owners, timing of returns, their magnitude and risks and others to determine the main and most important goal of the firm regardless of whether it is sole proprietorship, partnership or corporation. This goal will not only benefit the owners but as well as the managers and its employees. Therefore, the goal of the firm should be "to maximize shareholder's wealth". The following paragraphs will state related facts why I agreed that this is the appropriate goal of the firm.

Shareholders are the owner of shares of stock of the company in which that it can be any individual who is a holder of a stock. The wealth of shareholder is represented by stocks' share price. This means that if the price of the stock increases, the wealth of the owner goes up too, the same as with the value of the firm. I have the reasons to agree that maximizing shareholder wealth is the right and appropriate goal of the firm. This goal focuses on a long term approach where it aims to create wealth where cash flows and risk are the key decision variables. The job of the financial manager is to generate and bring wealth to the owners of the firm and makes financial decision in behalf of the shareholders. Whenever he thinks with regard of taking some action or decisions with increasing the share price of the stock, he should know when to accept or to decline the offer based on owners' best interest to have a good return.

For the reasons that maximization of wealth of the owner can be attained over a longer period of time, the benefits will be more likely positive and satisfying. Unlike with profit maximization, this is a short term goal and only concern about how much the company will earn at the end of the period without considering any kind of decision regarding the greater value of the company which is the value of the stock. However, maximization of profit is part of creating wealth in which present and prospective future earnings has taken into account and other factors that reflect the stock's share price. Each period, the company can see the growth and progress of the market share price of each shareholder's stock. It may take time before the company will earn a higher profit, the same that might experience losses. But in the long run, it will bring major earnings and develop strength of the firm in which its value will be greater than just maximizing profit as a main goal of the firm.

It is significant that wealth maximization considers the concept of returns and cash flows available to the stockholders, the same as risk factor. In this case, the financial manager can make decision in order to increase the price of the stock. For instance, greater cash flow normally resulted to a higher stock price. While in uncertainty, the stock price can be lower. If the shareholders take a certain degree of risk, the more they expect to get a greater return on their investment to satisfy the level of risk that has been generated. On the other hand, if the owners received a larger return, it can still be reinvested in the future to create higher earnings. Cash inflow and outflow and whatever benefits of returns or risk associated in this concept is the deciding element to determine the value of the firm because it is accurate information where you can see the outlook of financial condition and performance of the company. In accounting point of view, the in and out flow of cash in everyday operation is very important in making and planning decision in financial management. As discussed in chapter 3, it is stated that "cash flow is lifeblood of the company". Without this concept; it will be hard for a company to survive or become successful. That is why the financial managers should really carefully examine and plan both return and risk in order to accomplish the maximization of share price.

Furthermore, we have to take into consideration that the value of the return that has been produced in the first year could be more valuable in the years to come in which can be generally achieve in a long term. For this reason, the owners can be more satisfied because there is certainty on the quality of the benefit they will receive in the future. For instance, you just invested $ 200.00 stock at E-trade. After a few years, the value of that amount may be doubled, tripled or even more.

The job of financial manager will also include the interest of stakeholders, who are group of individual who plays a role in creating wealth maximization because they are the ones who have direct connection in the firm. There is no firm that would want to have a conflict with their employees. For example, if the company is looking after their interest, an employee is motivated and will show enthusiasm to work better which can lead to build up profits and accelerate cash flows of the firm. Moreover, they are the ones who deal with customers, suppliers, creditors and other members of the community who speaks about some new ideas, opinions, or suggestions about the company. Customer satisfaction is always necessary. If they feel that you value their business and show an appreciation with them, you can certainly get their loyalty. However, the goal is not to maximize the interest of stakeholders but to maintain to have a good relationship with them that will benefit to have a better decision to increase market share price over a certain period of time.

It is vital that a company has an appropriate goal which is shareholder's maximization of wealth in which requires the financial manager to protect the interest of stakeholders. Though, maximization of profit is not a main goal of the firm; this is a significant element to pursue in maximizing the wealth of the shareholders which can be achieve both in short or long term process, as well earning per share which indicates the future cash flows that continually shows the affect of share price.

Gitman, Principles of Managerial Management, 12th ed., New Jersey: Pearson, 2009.

What is bond's yield to maturity (YTM)? Briefly describe the use of a financial calculator, the use of an excel spreadsheet, the trial-and-error approach for finding YTM. Which do you prefer and why?

For a better understanding about yield to maturity, I would like to state how it relates with the bond which is another form of investment by an investor. Unlike holder of a stock who is one of the owners of the firm, you are the creditor if you are the holder of a bond. Bond is a long term credit instrument issued by corporation or by government as a means to raise big amount of money where the bondholder will receive an amount from the investment on the bond from a certain period of time called bond yield. The relationship between the yield and the bond is when you pay lower on the price of the bond; you will earn more earnings and with greater yield. On the other hand, if you pay more on the bond, your profit will be less and with lower yield. One of the three of most widely cited bond yield is yield to maturity.

Yield to maturity (YTM) is the rate of return that an investor will expect to earn in investing a bond with specific price allowing to hold until maturity date. This yield is associated with the current price of the face value of the bond and the yield gained in the form of coupon payments. In a simple thought, if the market current price of the bond is the same with the face value, the interest of the coupon rate is also the same. Moreover, if it is different from the face value to the bond price, the coupon interest rate will also be different. As I examined, yield to maturity compared with other type of yields is with more elaborated analysis of result of its calculation. In most cases, issuer is the one who prepared statement of all interest and principal payments. There are things to consider that it will be essential in computing yield to maturity such as current value (Selling price in the market that a buyer is willing to pay), face value (amount to receive by a bondholder at the time of maturity), coupon (interest paid which is usually semi-annually for the bond), and maturity (length of time before the face value will receive by the bondholder).

In calculating yield to maturity, you can use different types of computation tools. The most common ones are hand-held financial calculator, electronic spreadsheets, and financial tables as a help in computing a certain mathematical problem. Here, I will briefly describe the use of financial calculator, excel spreadsheet and trial and error approach in calculating yield to maturity.

Financial calculator. This is a device that is easy and convenient to use in solving any fundamental mathematical problem and financial matters. You will find primary keys to be use in solving a calculation. Normally, these calculators are programmed to compute the expected total which is typical in this type of instrument. With financial key functions, you will just enter the value on the appropriate boxes and it will give you the value that you are looking for. As long as you know the basic time value functions such as N, I, PMT, FV, PV, your computation for yield to maturity will make simple and quicker because one click of that key function will get the answer. For example, the bond price is $990.00 and face value is $1000.00 with 8 % coupon rate of interest pays semi-annually and 10 years of maturity. If you enter these values on appropriate key function, the yield of maturity is 8.15 %.

Electronic spreadsheet. Like financial calculator, excel spreadsheet have special built-in time value functions. If you have knowledge and skill in excel, this will be a simple and easy tool for you. At present, this is a very popular computing program in business especially in finance industry. Each individual cell has a formula or equation link to each of them. So if one of the values of variables is modified, you will notice the other cell solution will automatically change also. In calculating yield to maturity, any formula that can be use in excel will not always be exact rate of yield of maturity. On the other hand, you will have a practical and more explain value calculated because there is built-in formula with the equation to get the result. For the same example given, the spreadsheet will be like this and the yield of maturity is calculated as 8.15 %.

	A	B
1	Face Value	$1,000
2	Coupon Rate	8.00%
3	Years to maturity	10.0
4	Payment Frequency	2
5	Bond Price	$990
6		
7	Yield to Maturity	8.15%
8		
9	YTM is calculated as =rate(B3*B4,B2/B4*B1,-B5,B1)*B4	

Trial and error. This is a method of solving a problem of numerous attempts until you reach the desired result. In computing yield to maturity, this is a very useful method based on the bond's present value where if it has a higher value, the rate will be lower and vice versa. You just need present value interest factor (PVIF) and present value interest factor of annuity (PVIFA) in your computation.

It may take long before you can get approximate result but it is worth trying because it will give you a best estimate rate that you will anticipate to get until the maturity date.

.   All these three computation methods are effective in computing yield to maturity. Each of this method has an advantage and convenient way of calculating when circumstances needed. I always prefer to use excel in any of accounting problems such as computing yield to maturity I always prefer to use excel in any of accounting problems such as computing yield to maturity because I find it more effective to present the equation and the solution on how you got and derived the result. However, I would also like to use trial and error approach for comparison reason since I can do the computation differently until I get the expected rate of return.

        Yield to maturity is important concept for an investor because it helps them to compare and assess different bonds with irregular qualities, discount rates and prices in order to know how much will be the feasible return that an investor can expect on the maturity date of the bond. For this reason, investors can decide if it is a good investment.

Gitman, Principles of Managerial Management, 12th ed., New Jersey: Pearson, 2009.

Discuss NPV and IRR. Does the assumption concerning the reinvestment of intermediate cash inflow tend to favor NPV or IRR? In practice, which technique is preferred and why?

After the firm has settled relevant cash flows, the financial manager must determine which project is to be accepted or rejected. They are techniques in capital budgeting to perform this analysis which takes consideration the time value of money, time of project cash flows, their magnitude and risks, decision criteria on cost of capital and other related matters. The most preferred approaches are the two sophisticated capital budgeting technique namely: net present value (NPV) and internal rate of return (IRR).

Net present value (NPV) is a method to assess the profitability of a certain project calculated as the difference from the present value of cash inflows to the initial investment using a given discount rate. This rate is the project's smallest return to be acquired where the value of the firm will remain consistent. NPV is measured in currency which could be considered in the productivity of a project. Moreover, it gives the chance to evaluate the financial outcome of a business with regard to cost and revenue over a particular period of time. The decision criteria using NPV is: reject the project if the NPV is less than 0 and with negative NPV and accept the project if the NPV is greater than 0 and with positive NPV. With such acceptance of a project, it constitutes the value added to the firm, as well the market value of the owner's wealth. Thus, it considers time value of money and settles the risk of a project by applying the cost of capital as the discount rate.

On the other hand, internal rate of return (IRR) is an average rate of return at which NPV of an investment opportunity equals to zero. In simple words, it is the expected rate of return in an investment as in bond's yield to maturity. Financial managers use this method in making financial decision on a project calculated and measured in percentage instead of dollar amount. In terms of calculation, IRR involves a complex way of computation by trial-and-error approach. You have to calculate various discount rates until it equates the present value of the future cash flows of a project with the initial investment using financial calculator or excel spreadsheet. The decision rule using IRR is: accept the project if the IRR is greater than the opportunity cost and reject the project if the IRR is less than the opportunity cost. This rule assures that the company will acquire at most the required rate of return, as well increase the value of the firm and owner's wealth.

NPV and IRR have always the same accept –reject decisions for an independent or conventional project which normally provide the same outcome. However, ranking become critical when applying NPV or IRR method among mutually exclusive investments because it can produce conflicting results. This conflict is usually in different circumstances such as discrepancy in timing and magnitude of cash flow of a project. This means that the decision is based on one project to another in which cash flows; both in and out flow, may vary either increase or decrease over time or vice versa which resulted to one project to have greater NPV whereas the other project with greater IRR. Although the differences demonstrate conflicting ranking, the underlying reason of this conflict is that both NPV and IRR have an implied assumption about the reinvestment of intermediate cash inflows that are acquired before expiration of an investment. In NPV method, it implies that the cash flows of a project reinvested the expected rate of return or equal to IRR which is often higher rate than the opportunity cost.

Let me illustrate an example of NPV and IRR analysis:

	A	B	C
1		**Cost of Capital**	**8 %**
2		**Cash Flows**	
3	**Year**	**Investment A**	**Investment B**
4	**0**	-$4,600	-$4700
5	**1**	$3.200	$3,800
6	**2**	$1,500	$1,400
7	**3**	$1,700	$1,200
8	**NPV**	$998.49	$971.39
9	**IRR**	21.5%	22.3%

The NVP and IRR result is calculated with the use of excel spreadsheet. It appears in the example given that Investment A is the appropriate project using NPV whereas Investment B is IRR method. It is clearly shows that these two projects give a conflicting result which is likely because of the timing of cash flow or project's size and do not accordingly rank project in the same manner.

NPV and IRR are both useful and easy to calculate with help of computation tools. Certainly, it is not a simple job to choose which method is better with its distinct advantages and drawbacks. In most cases, financial managers and some investors help them to decide in terms of theoretical and practical view. Theoretically, NPV is considered to be sound correct and more realistic because the rate at which intermediate cash flow made by an investment is a rational estimate that could be actually reinvested at the cost of capital since IRR is oftentimes have a higher rate than the cost of capital in most of project. Likewise, NPV does not display certain mathematical properties that may create a multiple cash flows at distinct discount rates which arise from a project with a nonconventional cash flow pattern.

Despite of theoretical assumption of NPV, financial managers and investors prefer IRR method in practice. Basically, its consistency in calculation makes easier to analyze IRR with other rates supplied somewhere in the business market. In addition, it yields a percentage rate which tries to estimate benefits relative to the amount invested and apply it as a decision strategy to find out and determine the problems with the IRR.

In conclusion, NPV and IRR are important for evaluating project whether it will generate profit or losses for the firm. It is clear that NPV is effective with mutually exclusive project and IRR is often applied in individual or single project. Regardless of NPV and IRR preference, the financial manager should favor investments to good estimates of cash flow that are appropriate with maximizing the value of the firm and owner's wealth.

Gitman, Principles of Managerial Management, 12th ed., New Jersey: Pearson, 2009.

What is the relationship among operating leverage, financial leverage and the total leverage of the firm? Do these types of leverage complement one another? Why or why not? What is your preferred measurement?

In business, leverage is also an important concept for the progress and development of a company. This refers to the purchase of fixed assets and borrowed money to finance the business. The amount of leverage affects its value by the degree and irregularity of the company's overall risk and return. There are basic types of leverage that I would like to discuss. These are: operating leverage, financial leverage and total leverage.

Operating leverage is the capacity to use fixed costs operating a business to increase its affect of variability in sales on the operating profit or EBIT. It demonstrates the relationship between variable and fixed costs in a company's capital structure which is the mix of long-term debt and equity managed by the company. This means that operating leverage exceeds to a more than relative amount in change of operating income as a consequence of adjustment in the volume of sales. Oftentimes, the level of sales is the key element on the success or risk of any business. In other words, it is good when the sales revenue is increasing because the effect in the result of EBIT is higher. However, you can use to analyze operating leverage needed to cover all costs and the productivity related to the amount of sales by means of break even analysis. The degree of operating leverage (DOL) is measured and calculated by the percent change in EBIT from the sales. Operating leverage is present whenever DOL result greater than 1.

Let us see an example to show the EBIT for sales levels.

		Case 2		Case 1
Sales (in units)		750	1000	1250
Sales per unit price @ $12.00	$9000		$12000	$15000
Less: Variable costs @ $6.00	($4500)		($ 6000)	($ 7500)
Fixed costs	($3000)		($ 3000)	($ 3000)
Earnings before interests & taxes	$ 1500		$ 3000	$ 4500

In the example given, it shows that there is 25% increase in sales in Case 1 which resulted to 50% increase in EBIT whereas in Case 2 a decrease of 25% in sales and 50% decrease in EBIT. If you divide the percentage of changes as 50%/25%, it will result to 2.0 which means that the operating leverage is exist. The same result was calculated in a direct formula where the actual amount can be use.

Second type of leverage is financial leverage. It refers to the ability of a firm to earn more assets by the use of debts to increase the volume of sales and changes on earnings per share or EPS. It means that this debt will incur interest cost and payments of preferred stock dividends which will reflect on income statement of a firm. For this reason, the more debt of a company applies proportionate to its equity, the higher its financial leverage. The effect of financial leverage is that increases in EBIT will also an increase in EPS and vice versa. The degree of financial leverage (DFL) is the numerical measure which is calculated by the percentage changes in EPS from the change in EBIT.

Let us follow the given example previously to illustrate the EPS for EBIT levels.

		Case 2	Case 1
EBIT	$1500	$3000	$4500
Less: Interest ($500 annually)	(500)	(500)	(500)
Less: Taxes (30% bracket)	(300)	(750)	(1200)
Net profit after tax	$ 700	$1750	$ 2800
Less: PD (175 shares @ $4)	700	700	700
Earnings available for common	$ 0	$1050	$2100
Earnings per share	$0/1000= $0	$1050/1000=$1.0	$2100/1000=$2.10

In the example given, it shows that there is 50% increase in EBIT in Case 1 which resulted to 100% increase in EPS whereas in Case 2 a decrease of 50% in sales and 100% decrease in EPS. By dividing the percentage of changes to 100%/50%, the result will be 2.0. This means that the financial leverage is present.

The last type of leverage is total leverage. This is the combined of overall degree of leverage of a firm which is concerned in the relationship between the sales revenue and earnings per share. There will be total leverage if the firm has total fixed costs. So if the firm's level of total leverage is high, it will demonstrate the risk associated with it because there are more fixed costs in the company. The fact that the combined leverage is totally connected to the firm's operating and financial leverage, these types of leverage do complement each other in a manner that their outcome is a mere multiplicative and not additive.

This means that the overall outcome in the existence of these types of leverage is excellent, considering their combined leverage is relevant which magnifies the effects of changes in sales on earning per share. The degree of total leverage (DTL) is measured and calculated by percentage change in earning per share for a given change in sales. Like in operating and financial leverage, if the DTL is greater than 1, total leverage exists. If we take the previous example given above, the 25% increase in sales resulted to 100% increase of EPS which will give you the total leverage effect of 4.0. It is calculated as 100%/25% where you will get the same result in a more direct method.

I believe that the measurement of total leverage is better because it summarizes the combined outcome of leverage both, operating and financial. Hence, it can guide you to determine the most desirable level of financial and operating leverage, and as well the total risk that can be apply in leveraging aspects in capital structure of a firm by the use of effective ratio which show how much assets of a firm are sustained by a debt and by equity.

Leverage is useful when there is control in its level because it will demonstrate the advantage of using fixed cost assets and return source of capital that will help to increase the worth and value of a firm. Therefore, the financial manager should only consider major decisions concerning leverage and capital structure that are appropriate into the goal of the firm which is to maximize its share price and to reduce the risk of a company.

Gitman, <u>Principles of Managerial Management,</u> 12th ed., New Jersey: Pearson, 2009.

BUSINESS LAW

On April 19th, 1995, the Alfred P. Murrah Federal Building in Oklahoma City, Oklahoma was blown up resulting in 168 dead and over 800 injured. Three men were arrested for the crime, Timothy McVeigh, Terry Nichols and Michael Fortier. Prior to trial, the defendants requested that the trial be moved out of Oklahoma to another state. What would the court take into consideration when deciding whether a change of venue was warranted in this case?

A fundamental standard of U.S. law when the case will be tried in the United States is when the case will be heard where the crime was committed. This standard law is expressed in the manner of venue in which a place that the jurors will be chosen. Despite the courts is not totally in favor with forum shopping; it is essential that the case will be heard properly, fair and unprejudiced way. State or federal courts have different venue rules to where a case is to be heard. Normally, the proper venue for a trial is an appropriate location to conduct any legal action where the incident happens or where the defendant resides. In the case of Oklahoma bombing, the proper venue was considered in the city of Oklahoma where the incident was happened in which the defendants later requested the trial to move the trial to another venue. In this essay, I will discuss the factors that the court taken into consideration and warranted a change of venue outside Oklahoma.

Generally, a judge is opposed to allowing a defendant's request for a change of venue in a criminal case. For a reason, it is not only difficult for the parties of the case but also economically expensive. Nonetheless, a judge can order to move the trial to another location if he thinks that there is considerable proof of prejudice or unfairness on the defendant. This is not like a case in domestic relation about custody or child support which limits the request for transfer of venue or in a civil case in which an agreed venue is mainly on the convenience between the parties involved in the case.

The impact of the tragedy that has occurred in the city of Oklahoma in April 19, 1995 caused big sadness and grief in the heart of many particularly those who come from this place. I remembered the first time I heard this news when I still in Switzerland, I was shocked and asked myself that how a person could do such an evil act to a mankind. I became interested everyday what was the update on the case. If I am that enthusiastic on this case, it was much more to those in Oklahoma whom wanted to know the specific and detail information about the bombing especially those who are the actual witness and victim families of the incident. The consequences of this tragic event among the people of Oklahoma became a commonplace that they united as one family in the midst of this tragedy. For Oklahomans, the support and being part of the case was a means to surpass the grief and heartbreak and all emotional outcomes caused by this tragedy. However, this matter could be evenly conclusive proof that this case cannot have a fair trial in the area of Oklahoma.

On the other hand, the publicity of this case was becoming a nationwide subject. The focus of the media of the bombing from the very start was widespread news from the video footages, print news, television, radio and other forms of broadcasting. There was a massive amount of coverage regarding the scope of media on the blast, the arrests, the rescue recovery, victim and family interviews, investigations, court process and other related matters about the tragic event. With this pre-trial publicity, there could be an occurrence of assuming that this was a prejudicial publicity. The consequence of this matter could influence the opinion of the people particularly if the jurors chosen might be impartial and could not put aside of their feelings and beliefs brought by these publicity in which the defendants had been heavily accused. In such a case, the defendant has a constitutional right to have an appropriate and free from prejudicial trial and have the right to request a change of venue.

Additionally, Oklahoma displayed lacking and insufficient facilities of facilities. If these related facilities would be used in the court proceedings, it would cost a lot of money for renovation. At that point of time, it was not necessary for Oklahoma to spend such enormous expenditure for the propose renovation. Further if it was done, the time for construction would interrupt the court for scheduling the hearing date which would be generally unfair to the defendants. Even if this was not a major factor, I believed that this could be an added reason for the judge to decide whether to grant the request for change of venue.

Based on the summarized information where the connections of the people in Oklahoma on the case and the incriminating media coverage, it was proven that there would have great prejudice against the defendants and cannot acquire a fair and proper trial in the state of Oklahoma. As a question of law, though these defendants were committed the crime, they were still entitled to protection. For this reason, these were the considerations taken by the court in order to grant the change of venue in the bombing case in 1995 in another location outside Oklahoma.

---

1 Cheeseman, *Contemporary Business and Online Commerce Law,* 6th Ed. New Jersey: Pearson, 2009.
2 Lectric Law Library, *O.K. City Bombing Trial 2/96 Order Granting Change of Venue to Denver,* www.lectlaw.com.

The Sonny Bono Copyright Term Extension Act of 1998 granted individual copyright protection for their life plus 70 years. Do you believe that a period this long is necessary to encourage the production of creative work? What are the advantages and disadvantages of a longer copyright validity period?

When a certain original work that can be actually seen such as writings, films, paintings, music and other tangible form of things has been created and owned by an individual or any business, a form of legal protection can be given to the one who develop and build the work called copyright. It means that you are not only a physical owner but it protects your work from infringement or from the unauthorized use of it. The question is, how long does a work is protected by the law? A certain time has given to the creator of the work to have a copyright-protection. After the expiration of the copyright, the protection will be ceased and the work will allow the public to use their work as public property. In 1998, Sonny Bono Copyright Term Extension Act was enacted to extend the duration of the copyright period for their life plus 70 years. In this essay, I will discuss and examine if the longer copyright period is necessary to encourage the production of creative work as well its advantages and disadvantages.

We know that copyright is about securing the safeguard of one's author works and compensate them for their artistic effort. But copyright law has also acknowledged the interest of the public to use a priceless work. Since copyright is not permanent, a work will be a public property and everyone will have a free access to it. It is true that the objective of copyright is to inspire on their creativity by allowing the authors a right to have restrictions on substantial use of their works. Nevertheless, I think that this long period of time would not further encourage for work creativity.

While the author of the original work has an opportunity to gain more from it, the creativity will be held exclusively and limited just on the author of the work. So when he or she dies, his creation will be discontinued and could not have any opportunity to use or expand any creative ideas on this work by the public domain. Further, this piece of work could either lose or reduce the value of importance in the cultural history and would prevent the innovative activities of the present and future creators. When I started to paint for example, I was encouraged by someone's work. Through his painting, I had a chance to learn and recreate his work. Without any of this inspiration and free access, I would lose interest of pursuing or even trying it.

The longer copyright validity period would have advantages and disadvantages not only on an author's part but also to the public interests. This matter will show its circumstances based on some aspects. As I examined, I found that this longer period of copyright is not really beneficial at all to the public interests. Let us see how true this information in the following paragraphs is.

As it is important to compensate artists for their hard work on their creation, the creator will have longer time to earn profits for their work in which they can develop or pursuit more production. Because of this significance, they are more inspired to create further works so they can inherit them to their loved ones. However as I mentioned, the creative ideas on a particular original work will freeze up when the author dies and will slow or lose the economic value in the cultural heritage. The only person could benefit on the work left by the author will be the administrator of the copyright or the one who inherit the work whom probably would know nothing about the author's artistry.

On the other hand, what will happen if these works will be under the authorship of the owner of the work this long period of time? Can you imagine if Picasso, Van Gogh, Munch or Dali just died recently and their famous works will be frozen for a very long time? Aspiring or a student painter could not develop something new based on their works and it could not be more useful contribution in the general public. How about those students or an individual who wants to be a writer? They will have limited or could not enjoy the use of the materials without permission even if the original author is dead already. It is true that it will incentive the heirs of their work but the public will suffer cost to provide materials while it could be more beneficial for contribution to the public. Hence, it is difficult for them to provide material for their work with complicated agreement with the author that would result in greater cost to the public. As much that they could leave and pass it behind for his future generations, it would also be great if they could share their work to others and they could become an inspiration for those who aspire to be an artist whom its creation could be part and remembered in the cultural history.

In conclusion, I believed that the extending the copyright validity period this long would not be good because instead of encouraging the current or present creator, it would discourage them to boost new artistic creation. The heirs could have satisfactory and adequate period to appreciate the earnings already after the author has gone. After this period, it is time to make these works to have an important value as the basis of creating new works and significance to the general public to have a lesser cost.

Cheeseman, *Contemporary Business and Online Commerce Law*, 6th Ed. New Jersey: Pearson, 2009.

In many cases an incidental third-party beneficiary suffers a loss that can be directly traced to a party's breach of contract. Explain why incidental third-party beneficiaries are not able to recover their losses in such situations.

In a contract by law, the party can execute an agreement with the purpose of granting an advantage to an outsider in a contract. Whether its purpose is as a gift or to relieve from a lawful liability, a party that receives an advantage within a contract is a third-party beneficiary which can be either intended or incidental beneficiary. Although a party is not initially included in a contract, he or she might have the right to recover any losses arise from any breach of contract. However by rule, an only third party could enforce an action is the one who directly and intended beneficiary of a contract. In this essay, I will explain why incidental third-party beneficiaries are not able to recover any losses from its breach of contract.

When two parties formed a contract, they can settle an agreement to benefit a third party. The promisee should have an objective to benefit the third party while the promisor agrees to negotiate that the performance must be provided. The name of the third party would be identified in the contract as a direct beneficiary. Consequently, a contract would be clear that the he or she has a right to accomplish a legal action on this promise. In many situations, not all third-party beneficiaries have this right particularly the benefit was only obtained indirectly and unintentionally. This third party is known as incidental beneficiary. As a standard law, an agreement put into place by any government entity in a part of the group in the public are considered to be incidental beneficiaries. Essentially, they cannot obtain a judgment in a lawsuit from any government contracts, though they would endure some losses from a non-performance.

Let us take the example in the textbook where a third party was cited as an incidental beneficiary. The issue in Bain v Gillispie was to prove if the Gillispies were intended beneficiary of the contract between Bain and the Big 10 Basketball Conference. In this case, the court of record found that there was no legitimate issue on the evidence of Gillispie's demand that they were the direct beneficiary between the contracting parties. They were held to be not privy to the contract to either consider them as a donee or creditor beneficiary. Nevertheless, Gillespies could not contest about the issue because if there was a contract made between Bain and the Big 10, Gillespies could only be simply recognized as incidental beneficiary and they had no right to accomplish a legal suit against the original contracting parties. For this reason, the court affirmed dismissing defendant's counterclaim and sustained summary judgment.

As mentioned in the previous paragraph, it is not because a third party receives benefit from its performance would mean that you have the right with the terms and condition in a contract. Being an incidental beneficiary, you are not specifically named and identified as a direct beneficiary in an agreement. Despite a third party could accept an offer from a contracting party, the relationship of a beneficiary between them is not a direct one. This is the reason why he or she has no privilege in a contract and he or she cannot recover any damage brought by any nonperformance or breach of a contract.

Furthermore, I realized that one of the common cases that an incidental third party beneficiary usually comes into play is in a construction agreement. When our house was built, my parents had an agreement with an architect and a contractor at the same time. The contractor hired workers to perform services to construct our house. These workers would be the incidental parties between my parents and an architect's contract. This matter is an example that involves a third party in which cited many times in court in a case for breach of contract. Most of the times, contractors and subcontractors pursue losses and recovery from the construction project and claim that they are intended beneficiaries of the contract. But in fact, they are just simply incidental parties. In this type of case, a court is typically closely examines the basic contract in order to determine the argument of third party beneficiary in a matter before a court of law.

When a third-party beneficiary enters a contract, it is important to negotiate and review an agreement. It is essential to mention the intention of the parties to the third party and make sure that he or she has been given to perform something directly to the contracting parties with enforceable rights to a contract. Certainly as a third party, you would like to know your status in an agreement so it will be confirm that you are identified as either intended or incidental beneficiary.

Cheeseman, <u>Contemporary Business and Online Commerce Law</u>, 6th Ed. New Jersey: Pearson, 2009.

Is it reasonable for certain provisions of the UCC to apply to merchants only or to apply differently than non-merchants? Shouldn't anyone who choices to enter into commercial transaction be held to the same standard? Is it unfair to have two standards?

Every day, sellers and buyers deal with commercial business transaction. The Uniform Commercial Code was enacted to provide requirement in entering a sale contract and acknowledges an individual to enter an agreement according to their preference. This code will make easier in a more foreseeable and effective dealing in business. Article 2 of the UCC is a set of laws that relates to the sale of goods to meet the demands of both merchant and non-merchant while dealing with business contracts. Under this article, various provisions apply only for the merchants. The UCC treated them differently from the non-merchants because they are more experienced in dealing commercial transactions. Their specialization in dealing in sales makes it their profession. All matters related the sales of goods are their expertise. The non-merchant is just a typical consumer who wants to buy or sell goods without better understanding about details on commercial transactions. In order to make the subject matter clearly, I would like to discuss it further in the following paragraphs.

The Uniform Commercial Code is a code that applies to all sellers and buyers in a sales contract. These rules are a common set of rules requirement between contracting parties. As many of these rules deals with merchants, a stricter standard and requirements are set to follow from them than a casual buyer or seller. In Article 2 Section 104 of the UCC, the word "merchant" was defined.

72

They are the persons who buy and sell goods as their profession in which they have the ability to understand the concept involved in any commercial transaction. So if a contract is between merchants, the one who offer the sale of goods has an automatic obligation with additional condition made by the other party unless he or she refuses this additional condition in a contract. The UCC treated them with a higher standard that they are well knowledgeable about the course of their business practice. For this reason, a court could penalize them for nonperformance of a contract.

On the other hand, if a merchant deals with a non-merchant, he or she has a responsibility that a product sold will be under the compliance of the buyer. It means that if a merchant promise the buyer that the product is in good condition and no flaws. Then, this is what he or she should expect from it. A non-merchant does not have such duty to a merchant since he or she does not know about business standard in a commercial transaction. Thus, I would agree that certain provisions of the UCC apply for a merchant differently from a non-merchant.

Furthermore, part of a provision under the Uniform Commercial Code that all sellers and buyers have a duty of "good faith" in a performance of an agreement in sales. However, under the UCC, two distinct standards are involved in this code: a merchant standard and a non-merchant standard. For a non-merchant, the UCC provides the rule in Article 1 where good faith is considered as the honesty in any business transaction. An honest belief in an agreement made by a non-merchant would be sufficient to perform due to their lesser knowledge in a commercial transaction. In contrast with a merchant, honesty is not only a requirement in performance of a contract. But you also have to recognize an acceptable commercial standard of fair buying and selling practice. Consequently, I believed that an application of standard differently between a merchant and a non-merchant is just right and reasonable. If I sell for example my car to a person as a casual seller, I would not know all these requirements. As long that the buyer accepted my offer and paid the total amount of a car, the agreement was being fulfilled.

The status of a merchant in a business transaction is broader than a non-merchant. The UCC granted the merchants for more protection on the good sold or bought from another party. Further under the rule, four warranties involved in a commercial transaction are all applied to them while only two are for non-merchants. Nonetheless, merchants have more responsibilities to implement the provisions on the part of another party. Their knowledge in business dealings is necessary to comply those policies under Article 2 of the UCC in order to avoid any disputes. Hence, a court would examine closely to determine if a seller is a merchant for nonperformance of a contract.

I concluded that it is only fair that the Uniform Commercial Code have two standards. Non-merchant would not be able to understand all these rules with complicated information since they are just inexperienced seller or a buyer. However, it is only essential for the contracting parties particularly a merchant to any business transactions to be aware what rules to apply under this code in order to know if the performance and the requirements of its privileges have complied on the appropriate standard of care which accomplish an effective and lawful commercial transaction.

---

1 Cheeseman, *Contemporary Business and Online Commerce Law,* 6th Ed. New Jersey: Pearson, 2009.

2 Legal Information Institute, *Uniform Commercial Code,http://www.law,cornell.edu.*

PROJECT MANAGEMENT

Examine the keys to successful project portfolio management and analyze difficulties in successfully implementing this.

These days, a lot of companies are hard to find the significance of its project to achieve the strategies and goals of an organization particularly if a firm has several of projects for classification. With project portfolio management (PPM) which is a systematic method, an organization acknowledges to administer projects as an important plan to accomplish its objectives. Through this process, a project manager guide to manage and make decisions on the operation of a complex project. The only question is how an organization can carry out its implementation effectively. In this essay, I will discuss the keys to successful project portfolio management and its problem in implementing it.

The process of project portfolio management can be alarming but it can be attained by following the factors that contribute the success in selecting and assessing of a collection of projects. These factors are: flexible structure and freedom of communication, low-cost environment scanning, and time-paced transition.

The first factor is flexible structure and freedom of communication. If a company operates various projects, it is substantial to have the capability to change or create something in relation to a project existed already. In other words, if there is flexibility in the operation of the project without the restriction from layers of authority, it will have the chance to make original creative ideas for a project. Further, good communication is a vital step for effective application. So when there is a track of changes occurs in the operation of the project, the members of a team should give a clear and open communication to make sure that they are in the same pace to meet its portfolio's goals and objectives.

Low-cost environment scanning is the second factor. Nowadays, most of the companies focus their attention on a particular project that they think will lead them to success. This belief draws them to put all their time and ability to make it as a "home run" product in the market. This is sometimes beyond a thorough examination of market environment which is accomplish to check opportunities within its surroundings and the possible resources of a company that would be needed to increase these opportunities. Due to the quick changes occurrence and competition in the market, it is best to maintain with trends in their external environment. Through environmental scanning, an organization can try and create an original product successfully. For example, a company can test new products by giving a free sample. The right information helps to decide which product has more demands in the market before fully completing a certain product. For this reason, some companies do not really consider a "home run" approach.

The last and final key is time-paced transition. Due to quicker time to market, companies make changes from one product to another. But how it can be done effectively? Through portfolio management planning with a sense of timing, you have the chance to create a lengthy period and set actions beforehand for the product transition in an effective manner whether it is original or an improvement of an existing product. Many businesses have just succeeded in that matter like Gilette which has developed many new safety razors.

While administering project portfolio management successfully, there are challenges that may hinder its practices to become effective. According to the current study, the following areas are the most common issues in an organization.

1. **Conservative technical communities.** This matter occurs when there are strong disagreement between the senior management and the technical professionals of an organization. For example, a project engineer has a different opinion about a project that a management wanting to withdraw for a certain reason like it is very expensive to continue or not align with their objectives. Normally, a technical staff is hesitant to go along with this reasoning because they view that all projects are important.

2. **Out-of-synch projects and portfolios.** When a company starts to develop new strategic priorities, they still at times create new products that do not accord by its portfolio and it does not represent with the new strategic priorities for the company. Although, a project was executed effectively but if it does not provide the utmost value to the firm, it is still viewed as failure. To have a successful project portfolio, a project should always balance to its strategic goals so the time and money spent on this project would not be wasted.

3. **Unpromising projects.** One of the most typical issues in an organization is having lots of projects linked to their capability.

Consequently, a project manager could undermine which project that best characterizes to increase the value of the company's goals. Can you imagine that a project team will divide their time for these entire projects? How about the costs that a company will incur? It is significant for a project manager to discuss with the team which projects are more favorable particularly if a company has limited resources. It is a difficult task to stop a project that has started already but if it is not aligned with a company's strategy, it should be cancelled.

4. **Scarce resources.** If a company has too many projects in their portfolio but there is no enough availability of personnel, time and other insufficient resources to support these projects, it will certainly result in poor or inadequately executed project. Though a firm prioritizes a project but failed to allocate the resources appropriately, it is still a barrier to be successful. For example, if 5 people working on a critical project and also working on 6 other projects; they will not be able to concentrate this very critical project and its progress will be slower.

Project portfolio management improves the favorable outcome of projects because it brings an accomplished process of carrying out a course of action into projects and projects into business outcomes. A project manager should only follow the keys to implement it correctly with its strategy, the right project, and availability of resources and what proper things are to be done.

Pinto, Project Management: Achieving Competitive Advantage, 2ⁿᵈ ed., New Jersey, 2010.

Analyze the key differences between leaders and managers. Provide examples in your answer.

A company needs a manager and a leader to make it productively. You can be a manager and a leader at the same time or vice versa. They have agreeable characteristics connected to each other. However, they are distinct in concept and system of how a thing gets done to achieve its objective. A manager is someone in charge in a business operation of a company to attain its goal while a leader is someone who motivates or inspires somebody or a group of people to pursue an objective. They are number of ways differ a manager from a leader. In this essay, I will discuss further how they are different in the basis of creation of purpose, developing a network for achieving the agenda, execution, outcomes, and focus timeframe.

When it comes to a manner of working, a manager has a way of keeping the priorities of a company to achieve the best result. He has to perform a certain duties according to the rule and policy of a company. His/her focus of attention is the efficiency of a company's performance. This is to set a performance to plan, budget, and review the available funds and other functions of a management with his employees. For instance, you are a manager in a paper company; you have the task to make sure that the activities get done properly by your employees especially with deadlines on a daily operation of the business. On the other hand, a leader is not only a strategist but also a visionary who has clear ideas what would happen in the future. He brings this vision to the people to accomplish its goal. I would say a good example is Martin Luther King, a good leader who has a very interesting vision of the future.

There is a different way in developing a system on how to achieve a certain goal between a manager and a leader. A manager assigns a certain responsibility to the employees. With this appointment, he has to assure that the progress of their task at hand will be monitored towards job accomplishment. As an employee, for example, I have to obey what my manager asks me to do to complete a job on time. In contrast, a leader does not need to assign the people what to do. Instead, he relates and communicates to the people. He does not have to hold a management skill in order them to follow him. All he needs to gain their supports is addressing his concern and make them understand why things are vital to be done. Martin Luther King Jr. had just done that by sharing his vision to the people.

Managers and leaders manage an execution in a different manner. Managers keep the system in good condition and efficiency of the business. It means that it has to be certain that all things are performed properly. So when a problem occurs, a manager has to deal with it at hand and take best corrective measure to accomplish the result. For instance, if a company has a conflicting issue between two employees, a company has to do something to resolve this issue immediately. On the contrary, a leader is more concern about accomplishing the vision. Wherefore, it is ordinary to experience any problems or issues that must be dealt and work it together. Further, he encourages his team or the people that it is better to think what favorable impact could bring this with them rather than standing by a company's policy.

A manager and a leader are two different people with vitality and shortcomings. Usually a manager is satisfied on the current standing of a company especially when it is very successful. He is good in keeping up status quo which hinders change. A manager avoids risk and focus on outcomes on a shorter period of time. Whereas, a leader is an innovator and do not abide in status quo. Through change, they believe that there is a continued development or opportunities for success in the future. For instance, Martin Luther King encouraged the people to change. He was not afraid to take a risk to accomplish his goal for a long period of time until his death. If you will never try or risk anything, you would not know what would be the outcome to reach your goal.

Let me show a summary of an easy method to demonstrate the difference between a manager and a leader. For example, our office will be hosting a charity event. The following table shows the duties of a manager and leader to attain this project successfully.

Manager	Leader
1. Plan the charity event and determine the things to be decided such as budget and cost necessary for the event.	1. Set the objective of holding a charity event.
2. Accomplish the plan and monitor its progress.	2. Determine how to achieve its goal.
3. Set up a team and assign duties to them.	3. Encourage and persuade the team why they have to be a part of this event.

4. Oversee the team and ensure that they perform their tasks properly. Overcome any obstacles. For example, the place is not available for the event.	4. Check the development and make sure that the team is focused towards a common goal. If a problem occurs, they will work it out together.

In conclusion, it is true that being a manager is you intend to do the things right in a business while a leader is to do the right thing. This demonstrates that they are two different characters. Nevertheless, they are both evenly significant in the strength of a company. If managers and leaders recognize their capacity and relate to each other it will give the opportunity for the company to be successful.

Pinto, <u>Project Management: Achieving Competitive Advantage</u>, 2nd ed., New Jersey, 2010.

Examine the different approaches to building a project budget and explain why would one be used over another.

A company without a financial plan on each function is putting a business at risk of deficiency because a budget is part of project manager's preparation and administering the entire operation of the business. So to create a project budget effectively is a very important aspect of project management which is often aimed to incorporate organizational objectives, appropriation of resources and other related activities as characterized in the Work Breakdown Structure (WBS) to make the project costing efficient. This activity is a great challenge for a project manager who should have the skill at keeping the estimates of the cost of a project precise and correctly. To attain this process, there are two common approaches utilize by a company which I will discuss in this essay. These are: top down and bottom up budgeting.

Top-down Budgeting

Top-down requires the actual input from the upper management to a lower department of a company which begins the course with a flow of data based on their assumption with a previous project that are similar. Once the approximate computation of the total amount has been established, it will be breakdown into specific details between the smaller components of the Work Breakdown Structure until these amounts will be assigned to all work packages. This means that the team actually perform the project will work the best of their capacity one task at a time within the allocated amount. For example, I have a task to clear a 10000 square feet land. The approximate cost that will be used in this activity is $ 1,400.00. This amount will be divided and break down into segments such as labor cost for clearing the lot, rental cost of equipments and other fees to work this task.

As much as bottom up approach is very common, there are companies that are comfortable in using a top down approach. For this reason, the allocation of a fund for a project at the start of the process could be compelling on the use of the resources and have a better outcome to achieve its objective. Likewise, it will be difficult for the employees to maintain the essential resources to accomplish its organizational objectives because the higher management who set up the budget does not really know the related expenses of each department. As an employee, for instance, I could be more inspired and motivated to perform my task in an effective manner if I am part of the budgeting process.

Bottom Down Budgeting

Bottom down is a traditional budgeting which is a different approach from the top-down. The budget starts from the lower level department to be proposed for an approval at the highest level of an organization. Although a manager completes the project budget, its team has direct input during each level and prepare an allocation of a fund for each function that supports the activity. If the plan have not approved, they have to modify it until the top management agreed with it. This approach has detailed information on how the budget is developed. Let us take a look on how it works. First of all, you need to determine what activity required to accomplish a project so the cost could be estimated. For each work package, compute the amount of direct and indirect cost until you derive with the total cost where it can be done from working one task to another. For example; begin to budget the project weekly, then monthly until you approach to annually. So if the cost for a week is $1,000.00. The monthly cost would be $4,000.00 and the total cost for a year would be $48,000.00

Bottom up have used by many firms. Normally, the managers are more acquainted with segments in operating level so the estimated costs tend to be accurate as long that no task has been missed out. Since the employees are involved in the process, they are more motivated to perform their job well. Moreover, it will enhance a good communication among the member of an organization. Nevertheless, there are a number of drawbacks in this approach. The time and amount required in budgeting plan would be a factor. At bottom up, the upper management decreases the control over the budget. In this case, they have concern about over spending because it might not able to use the fund wisely. For the reason that this approach need to make a complete list of activities to fulfill a project, it is hard to maintain its accuracy which may lead to miscalculation. Further, the management concerns about the time allotted to work on this process might be a waste great deal of time. Maybe, managers have good information about the needs of each department but with less knowledge about its strategic goals and objectives of a company.

In summary, I believe that in order to substantiate a firm organizational goal and preference of a company, it would be better for a project manager to have collaborated with these two approaches. Usually, the combination of using top down and bottom up is necessary in some specific cases that will help a breakthrough development to achieve its strategic goal.

Pinto, Project Management: Achieving Competitive Advantage, 2nd ed., New Jersey, 2010.

Identify the concerns that arise when shutting down a project. Examine which are the easiest and most difficult to address.

Normally, all project should carry on until accomplished and completed with all output expected by satisfied customers and clients. Nonetheless, the outcome of some cases is not the same as they anticipated. Hence, a project may be cancelled even before it is entirely completed. Terminating a project at an earlier stage is one of the most crucial decisions that a management can be made. At this point, it can be hard and very complicated to deal by the project managers because some challenges and problems can be faced before and after shutting down a project which is necessary by a company to be settled. These issues are divided into two categories which I am about to discuss in this essay. These are emotional and intellectual issues.

Emotional problems occur to the members of a team and their clients. When a project has been terminated earlier, one of the worries of the team are losing their job and would not have reassignment of duties to another project. Oftentimes, the team gets lost their initiative to work effectively and perform their job poorly in the remaining activities to be done. In addition, there is no more sense of unity among the team members where the goal to develop and achieve a favorable project has been lost. Some of the team changes their path of engaging a new project to a better opportunity while others have concerns regarding who will be chosen to reassign in another project.

Another emotional issue occurs to the clients. Usually, if the project is being terminated, there could be a possibility that the clients will change the way they think and hesitant about the project. They might view the shutting down a project as a failure so they may not want to be involved in any coming projects. Further, they might change their staff that does not have knowledge about the project at this critical period. As a result, personnel that have the ability to provide expertise regarding the project are no longer accessible.

The second category of concern is intellectual issues. This category deals with internal and external issues of a terminated project. Let us start with internal issues. Following the termination, the team member should identify in which of the project deliverables have been satisfied and what has not been finished in which I believe it is not easy to deal with. Also, requiring a certification in conformity in the cause of a project cancellation should be done as part of the process. Recognize all unresolved commitments such as supply contracts and deliveries which should be dealt with care and attention. When a project shuts down, it is necessary that all accounts should be close to stop somebody who has the interest in hiding it. Another issue that a project manager addressing is to evaluate what activities or tasks that are still remaining but not related or necessary anymore to the growth of a project should have to be eliminated. Once this process is fulfilled, then it can be consistently closed those work orders and packages with their permission to stop from incurring added charges. All materials that will not be used any longer should be transferred to the head office for inventory. Sometimes, they convert it into cash by selling to regain the residual value of it or either it can be placed something useful like recycling.

On the other hand, external issues are more challenging which deals with unresolved problems with clients, contractors, suppliers or vendors as it requires settling it directly particularly if there is a claim on to them. The project firm should make an arrangement with the suppliers for the remaining deliveries and contract termination. Further, good communication with the closure is vital to all the members of the team, clients and all individuals involved in the project. This will help to avoid any cause of problems that might occur to this stage. When the arrangement from the clients has been obtained and all tasks have been fulfilled, shutting down the building or place of operation should be done within scheduled time. Finally, the last important thing to be done whether the project has been accomplished or cancelled is the post project audits depending on the specification of the members of the team and the clients. This evaluation will be helpful for a project manager to make it better and avoid the flaws made and how it can be prevented on the next project.

The most difficult stage of project life cycle is closing out a project. There are easiest and difficult to deal with on these concerns and issues that I mentioned in the previous paragraphs. Certainly, the difficult one is associated directly on the project team and the clients. The emotional issues among them affect the accomplishment of the remaining project. Tension and worries take over them that pulling them away from achieving the remaining tasks to be done. The same challenges encounter with the clients during this period in which the project manager should address carefully. Further, one of the hardest to manage is the concerns that categorize in external intellectual problems because it requires an immediate resolution or settlement. For example, if a client has to claim against the project organization, it will be a huge issue if a project manager does not have the capability of eagerness to settle a resolution to the problem and negotiating knowledge. This will lead to a major legal dispute even after the project termination. In addition, a project manager must be completely knowledgeable with the controlling documents and the quality of work accomplished to that point.

However, the easiest issue to address is mostly on the internal intellectual issues. It can be easier because the project team can still resolve the issues as part of the closeout procedure. Once the issues have been analyzed and described to resolve their final arrangement, some of them might not be appropriate anymore and can be disregarded.

Although shutting down a project can be done in a lesser orderly manner and a limited closeout procedure, a project manager's comprehension on his team members and client's concerns can be useful in connection with the closeout process. In this case, this knowledge of emotional issues may obtain an agreeable motivational outcome of them to accomplish the remaining project. Thus, the success by recognizing this matter can greatly facilitate the manner to address intellectual problems that are to be settled.

Pinto, *Project Management: Achieving Competitive Advantage*, 2nd ed., New Jersey, 2010.

STRATEGIC MANAGEMENT

Give at least seven reasons why some firms do no strategic planning.

In business, strategic planning is a useful tool to bring the company a guide to achieve goals or objectives into success and decision making on the day to day operation. Many companies engage in this activity so they can have an idea if their business is going to be a successful in the future. As much that it has benefits that it can contribute for the progress of any firm, there are still some firms avoiding it. Some company does not think that it will guarantee to bring a business into success or what will happen in the future. Although, some firms engage to do this process but if without or little support from the members of the organization, it will certainly fail.

In this essay, I would like to discuss the seven reasons which I would explain further in the next paragraphs why some firms do no strategic planning. These reasons are: waste of time, too expensive, laziness, prior bad experience, fear of failure, fear of the unknown and firefighting.

The strategic planning is a complex process that it will take a lot of time and effort before it will be properly implemented which involves compiling, analysis or evaluation of information and documents. Once you started to plan, you should move forward and continue it. Otherwise, the valued time contributed in establishing a strategic plan could be wasted especially if setting up their objectives is not accomplished adequately. Consequently, some firms view this as a waste of time in particular if all the time spent in the process lead to nothing.

The process of strategic planning is too expensive that it will cost thousands or even millions of dollars particularly for a big company. This case does not make a sense for a small or non-profit company who oppose to spending money for that matter. Normally, you have to hire professionals who are specialized in this field to perform the planning in order to formulate and implement it properly. In addition, some firm's professionals and experts will also be sharing their time where they will be paid extra for their services. Some firms consider that this planning is just an expense rather that a tool to make the business grow and improve. Oftentimes, when they started the plan, they run out of budget. It may happen because maybe they do not have the appropriate or allocated budget of resources for this purpose. For this reason, a company prevent from doing it.

In strategic planning, teamwork is needed among the managers and employees of a company. You may ask yourself, how can I be a part of this activity? Moreover, the managers should have the acceptance of forming it in order to motivate their employees to work with eagerness to achieve their goals. If the manager is the first person who does not have the effort and willingness to formulate the plan, it will not work. It is worse if the employees do not have the commitment and longing to be involved in the application of the strategic planning. If this is the case, a company might just avoid doing it due to laziness of the members of an organization.

One of the most common worries that affect the decision in formulating a strategic plan is fear of failure. Every businessman would want their firm to succeed. Unfortunately, if it comes to their mind that there will be a chance of failure, they would rather not to do it at all.

When the first time the company formulated and implemented the strategic plan and it was not successful, it will likely that the next one will tend to result the same. They have fear the previous bad experience with strategic planning will happen again. For instance, they hired a poor consultant or planner who happened to damage their company. Or maybe, the time that they consumed in formulating the plan did not really achieve anything or some unpleasant situation occurred during that time. I could understand that due to this matter, a company may not want to repeat the same mistakes and troubles they had before.

When changes occur in a firm due to implementation of a strategic plan, some manager feels to be pressured in which it can lead to fear of the unknown. This can cause employees' concern on their skills and the ability to adapt the new structure of a company particularly if a manager moves them from one task to another. This position will make them frustrated and confused on their working abilities to the change that might be resulted in poor performance on the fulfillment of the strategic plan.

Finally, firefighting is the last reason. It is usual for many companies to have management issues and managing its operational activities in which they are busy dealing with every day. This thing becomes an excellent excuse for them to hold back strategic planning. A manager or an employee might complain like "How can I have time for strategic planning, I even have problems with my job right now. I do not want more troubles." There is no company would wish a business is in conflict and complaints among its members so they think that strategic planning would not be a good idea.

In conclusion, the strategic planning is a systematic way that can help the business of a firm in seeking favorable circumstances to achieve the benefit to stay of being competitive. However, I believe that the planning process can be done according to the flexibility, size, financial status or what product and services offered by an organization. I would think that it is better to plan rather not does it at all. It might be critical and hard for the first time but with patience and discipline, you will most likely be able to know what your business will become and where it will be going.

David, <u>Strategic Management: Concept and Cases</u>, 12th ed., New Jersey, 2009.

What four basic steps comprise the controlling function of management?

In any type of business, function of management is important that describes how a manager performs in a business organization to attain their goals and objectives in a satisfactory manner. The controlling function is one of the five activities in a management. This is a process to guarantee that the existing function is in conformity according to the established standards by a company. It obtains basic precautionary measures to decrease incompetence where a manager may be assessed in this task. It consists of four basic steps in order to have effective strategy evaluation in controlling function management. Here are the basic steps that I would like to illustrate further as follows:

1. Establishing performance standards
2. Measuring individual and organizational performance
3. Comparing actual performance to planned standards
4. Taking corrective actions

Let us talk about the first step. It is significant for a company to develop criteria to be used to measure the performance. With these standards, it becomes easier the process of controlling management. It is only necessary that it should only be precise and clear statement of usual outcome of a service, product, cost, profit, individual, production or sold units so it would be clear to members of an organization. In a publishing company, for example, the minimum number of books to print is 25 units per order. So the established standard is 25 books. Establishment of standards can determine the level of performance of each employee or an organization. For this reason, it will help them to comprehend what a company anticipates on what they can do and how it will assess their work accomplishment.

The next step after the standards has been established is measuring performance. In this step, a manager should direct the employees accordingly and motivate them to carry out their job efficiently. In this manner, a manager would be able to discover the flaws and mistakes of the performance in every phase of production where it will have the opportunity to use appropriate action to resolve the issues existed in an organization. For instance, if the standard unit of their production is 500 per week but they only produced 400 units, a company should act upon to increase it per week. There are ways that can be done to measure performance either tangible or intangible such as written or oral reports, statement, behavior or performance evaluation by an individual, selling or production outcome and others.

The comparison of an actual from standard performance is the third step in controlling in an organization. This means that a manager has an obligation to find out if the actual performance has met the outcome with anticipation and assure that there is compliance with standards agreed upon by an organization. However, a manager should exercise exception to the rule. In this matter, a manager should discover if the deviation existed from the standard is whether critical or acceptable for a business. It means that if it is critical, a company should act on it accordingly because this will affect the operation of a business. On the contrary, if it is acceptable, there is not much of a concern to do something. Let us say, for example, a firm has a deviation between issues of equipment that has broken and a 5% increase in the cost of office supplies. It is necessary to take immediate action replacing broken equipment in order to resume operation of a business while an increase of 5 % on office supplies is less significant and can be disregarded.

The final step is taking corrective action. In this step, a manager will show the cause of deviation and take a proper remedy to solve any bad circumstances occurred in an organization. Oftentimes, these issues can be easy and difficult to resolve depending on the cause of the problem. As cited in the previous paragraph, for example, the manager learned that the reason why the workers produced under the standard units is because of their workers laziness and slow to perform their job. In this matter, a manager may have to dismiss and replace them from their work and hire those who can do their tasks quicker and attentively.

After evaluating the condition of a business, a manager is required to take corrective measures to these negative issues. At times, this process may involve modifications of activities such as a better hiring process, choosing efficient machines, or the more regular group analysis and others. These actions should be done immediately and appropriately to prevent these issues in the future. But sometimes, instead of changing a certain function, revision of the original standard is the best solution to fix the problem.

In conclusion, controlling is one of the most significant process of an organization which is linked to planning. It requires regular results finding out important range of the incompetence of a business to enhance general performance so it can accomplish the goals and objectives that have desired by a company. In other words, even if you have a good organizational plan but without control of it, a manager cannot recognize its achievements. The plan can only be accomplished with proper controlling which is necessary if you want to have a productive and effective business.

David, <u>*Strategic Management: Concept and Cases*</u>, *12th ed., New Jersey, 2009.*

Compare and contrast the five types of bankruptcy.

It is a responsibility of an individual or any business to pay their debts. However, what happens if you cannot be able to furnish anymore a payment on your indebtedness. In this circumstance, the government created a federal law to protect a debtor from a creditor on their outstanding debts known as bankruptcy. In this way, a creditor will be prevented to sue a borrower who could be eventually a debt-free on his or her past credit obligation. In this essay, I will describe under the U.S. Bankruptcy Code the differences and similarities in the following five types of bankruptcy:

1. Chapter 7- Liquidation
2. Chapter 9- Adjustment of Debts of a Municipality
3. Chapter 11- Reorganization
4. Chapter 12- Adjustments of Debts of a Family Farmer or Fisherman
5. Chapter 13- Adjustment of Debts of an Individual with Regular Income.

Chapter 7 is a type of bankruptcy commonly called as liquidation. Among the other types of bankruptcy, this is the simplest and quickest process which can be filed by an individual or any business. Nonetheless, you should have a lower or no income in order to be qualified. Or else, chapter 13 is the best alternative where an individual or business can also file. Just like chapter 12, 13 or even in some cases in chapter 11, a trustee will be appointed by a court who administers to sell non-exempt properties to pay the creditors. The process usually takes a shorter time before you will be released from your debts. The reason is because there is no repayment plan involved in the process and there is a liquidation of debtor's properties and assets to pay debts to the creditors as compared to the other four chapters of bankruptcy in which it will take normally 3 to 5 years of process.

Chapter 9 is the second type of bankruptcy which is mainly applies to municipalities. This is quite similar to chapter 11 because they are both reorganization. Nevertheless, chapter 9 is designed specifically for adjustment of debt of a city, town or a county while chapter 11 is for commercial businesses. As to reconstructing their debts, a repayment plan must be filed and affirmed by a court similar to chapter 11. Further, due to a bigger size of a group to be involved in this bankruptcy, the course of action can be more complicated. There is also a trustee assigned in chapter 9 but it has limited tasks as compared to chapter 11 where there are more duties assigned. The big difference of chapter 9 from other chapters is that the case has no alternative for transfer to other bankruptcy types because of its uniqueness in eligibility to file.

The third type of bankruptcy is **chapter 11** which is known as reorganization. As mentioned in the previous paragraph, it has similarity with chapter 9 in terms of reconstructing their debts. With chapter 11, it does not have limits in terms of the amount payable by the borrower as compared to other bankruptcy types like chapter 13 which has a cap on amount in secured debts of less than $350,000 and unsecured debts of less than $100,000. Among other bankruptcies, this is the most expensive in the cost of filing and has a considerable difficulty in the process. Instead of discharging its debts to the creditor, the debtor reestablishes its business operation into productivity while they can still repay their debts.

The bankruptcy that applies exclusively to family farmers or fisherman is **chapter 12**. In order to be eligible, you must have a regular or steady income. In many ways, the procedure is kind of similar to chapter 13 such as the borrower can arrange for payment of their debts for a period of time from 3 to 5 years. For this reason, debtor's business can stay in operation while repaying their debts. The differences are: only a farmer and fisherman are eligible to file it and it has a higher cap amount of its debt than in chapter 13. There is also a trustee with similar tasks as in Chapter 7 or 13 assigned by a court. A debtor can keep away the creditors from his possessions or assets but he is obliged to pay his debts in his prospective incomes.

The last type of bankruptcy is **chapter 13**. Like in Chapter 7, this is used by an individual or a business. In spite of some similarities with chapter 7, the process in chapter 13 is broader and longer. You should have a regular or higher income in order to qualify and the amount of debts will not exceed under the Bankruptcy Code. There are reasons why an individual or a business prefers chapter 13 to file their bankruptcy rather than chapter 7. One reason is because there is no liquidation of property and assets. It means that you can keep what you have such as home or car same as in chapter 11 and 12. For example, if you are still paying a mortgage in your house or installment payment on your car, it will be saved from seizing it, and you can still pay your debts through your monthly salary in which repayment plan will be proposed and approved by a court. Unlike chapter 7, the period of discharge will take longer between 3 to 5 years.

Bankruptcy could be use effectively as a retrenchment strategy of a company or an individual. However, filing a bankruptcy is a serious matter that will damage your credit score and will have a considerable consequence on your finances for a very long time. It is only significant for an individual to learn how these types of bankruptcy could affect on them. For this reason, we could able to prevent it with a more suitable decision making in our financial matters.

1David, *Strategic Management: Concept and Cases*, 12th ed., New Jersey, 2009.
2Legal Information Institute, *U.S. Code: Title 11-Bankruptcy*, *http://www.law.cornell.edu/uscode/text/11*.

What are the three commonly used strategies or approaches changes in an organization? Give an advantage and/or disadvantage for each type of approach.

In today's economy, most of the companies enforce to have organizational change in order to keep up the business to be productive and competitive in the market. Unfortunately, this strategic management approach is not an easy task for all the members and the entire organization. Regardless in what manner they look it, it will certainly bring them confusion and cause trouble in communicating about the change. Like a management planning, there are reasons why they resist changing. The common concern is that they are afraid to lose or transfer their jobs or they fear that they cannot adapt the change or new structure of a company. This is the reason that a resistance from change cannot be avoided. The following approaches or strategies are the commonly used to manage resistance change.

1. Force change strategy
2. Educative change strategy
3. Rational or self-interest change strategy

The first approach that I would like to discuss is force change strategy. This approach places emphasis on using power to force an individual to comply with the change management. When you are in power, an authority to demand your employees applying the new system of a company can be significantly beneficial because they have no alternative but listen and abide by it. If the employees would not conform to the change, a company might apply threats like demoting from your position, no chance for promotion or even worst, you might be fired. It can be unpleasant means of getting them to follow it but sometimes, it is a necessary action since time factor is vital for an organization. However, there is a drawback in this approach. Normally, the employees or those affected by the change would have felt hurt or angry because it does not acknowledge their opinion or concern about the change. It may be done the implementation promptly but the employee's commitment to it could be longer due to the high resistance of cooperation or they might simply quit their jobs.

The educative change strategy is the second approach. In contrast with the previous approach, this is more informative to persuade an individual or group of people on the call of change. In this way, they might switch their ideology and attitude differently and a tendency to be able to support it. It is important that the ones affected by a change are their acceptance and commitment to it. Knowing the significance of a change, they will be more considerate. The information that they need to know about it will help them to understand why change has to take place which can stimulate them for a longer commitment. Collaboration between the employees and the management to implement the change is necessary in order to be working this approach. Nevertheless, it can be difficult to manage it particularly if it involves a lot of employees. Moreover, the implementation will take a longer and a lot of patience should be needed.

Finally, the last strategy is rational or self-interest change strategy. In order to achieve the purpose of this strategy is to give them a reason that this will be beneficial and bring good to them. Although at times, it does not have a favorable circumstance on some members of an organization, I always view change as an advantage because I can learn more and I could use this new skills and knowledge in the future. For example, we will have a new system in our office. It is necessary for all the employees to have a two months training before we can implement the new system. It is clear that it will take longer to accomplish it and would be costly too. However, if this strategy succeeds, the implementation would be comparatively simple and the involvement will lead to a longer commitment to it.

Among the three approaches, the rational or self-interest change strategy is the most appropriate. According to Jack Duncan, it consists of the following four steps in order to make it work.

1. A manager should provide the employees the opportunity to participate and involve in its process. In this case, they can recognize their one's own advantage in the change. So if their opinions and views taken into account, they will have greater commitment to achieve the change.
2. One way to motivate the employees to be part of the change is to present them with incentive or reward.
3. It is important to communicate with the employees and make them understand why the company is in need of change.

4. A manager should have feedback or information how the process of change has been doing within an organization where employees will certainly appreciate it.

Where there is organizational change in a company or organization, resistance from its members are a common reaction that should be expected. It is only vital that the related information about the change should be properly informed ahead of time to the ones most affected. It is true that it can be necessary to emphasize their involvement so they will feel part in the process to reach for a common goal. Maybe, they see a change as neither negative nor positive but the most important is that their feelings and views about it are taken into consideration. For this reason, resistance could be minimized and easier to manage by a manager who is responsible to motivate the employees and use appropriate strategy to overcome its resistance.

David, <u>Strategic Management: Concept and Cases</u>, *12th ed., New Jersey, 2009.*

MARKETING MANAGEMENT

Good mission statements are essential to being a success in business. Describe the three major characteristics that good mission statements should have.

Mission statements are statements that organizations develop to share with managers, employees, and (in many cases) customers. This statement will show the reason why businesses exist and will accomplish and guide through the success of the business. Normally, an organization reflects on the vision of the business in relation on the purpose of its existence, and sense of direction and opportunity to look forward on the future of the company. For example, co founder of Sony, Akio Morita wanted that he could bring to the people to have "personal portable sound". For that goal, the company created walkman and CD player which is later updated to a more advance technology like wireless sound system or mp3. Sony has become one of the most successful and prestigious company in the world. Now we can ask a question, how we can have a good and effective mission statement? By the textbook, it consists of five major characteristics. These are: focusing on limit goals: stressing on company's major policies and values: defining major competitive spheres: taking a long term-view: and being short, meaningful and memorable as possible. To explain the three of each characteristic, I will take example of a mission statement stated as follow:

Rubbermaid Commercial Products Inc.:

"Our Vision is to be the Global Market Share Leader in each of the markets we serve. We will reach this leadership position by providing to our distributor and end-user customers innovative, high quality, cost-effective and environmentally responsible products. We will add value to these products by providing legendary customer service through our Uncompromising Commitment to Customer Satisfaction."

First, stressing on company's major policies and values. Certainly, mission statement is something that a customer raises a question such as, why I am going to have business with you? The core values and beliefs of the business help to motivate the employees to work together especially when it comes to customer satisfaction. As we examine the example given, the value of the business is "providing legendary customer service through our Uncompromising Commitment to Customer Satisfaction." In doing so, they will reach the leadership position as the company will become the Global Market Share Leader. Also you will notice that their policy is to serve their customers with high quality, cost-effective and environmentally responsible products. Here we could see that their commitments and motivation to work together will inspire them that their work is significant to achieve the goal as they serve their customers satisfactorily.

The second characteristic is defining major competitive spheres: These are: industry, product and application, competence, market segment, vertical, and geographical. These competitive spheres define on how and what the company will operate. Let's check the example given and I will analyze it with major competitive spheres as follows:

- Industry. Rubbermaid offer environmentally responsible products for commercial and industrial markets and more product categories that have been manufactured in their international based branch. This company is set for one or more industry.

- Products and applications. Their brand name will clearly tell you what their products are made and consist of. Their aim is to provide their customers with high quality, cost effective and environmentally responsible products.

- Competence. This company is continually expanding and updating new and substantial products for better use to offer for their customers and best practices, as strong and successful partner.

- Market segment. Rubbermaid wish to serve the market globally based products for commercial and institutional markets such as food categories, home and safety product.

- Vertical. Rubbermaid started to produce and sell a line of plastic home products in U.S.A but their channel of level of organization as well its distribution is getting bigger as they have established offices based abroad.

- Geographical. Rubbermaid becomes multinational company. The company operates in many countries in the world such as in Europe and Asia.

Lastly, mission statement should be short, meaningful and memorable as possible. What does it mean? It is use in simple chosen word or language that is specific with meaning. You do not want your customer have trouble understanding what does it meant. It should be convincing and compelling for the customers' action to buy as well. Expressing vision is also an option to include in the mission statement which could be meaningful. It indicates that it will grow, stabilize, and plans more strategies in the future for the success of the business. In my opinion, the example given is just as clear and short statement with what they wish to offer to their customer as well as their organization. I wouldn't change a word on it.

No matter how hard the tasks in order to have a successful business, it is necessary to complete your mission statement based on the criteria on how to have an effective and good mission statements. If that is the case, I believed that you will reach your goal and purposes to meet the demands and need of the customers and the members of the organization to achieve the goal that is hope for the business. In addition, good mission statement will result to a promising experience and relationship within an organization, partners, or customers and others in relation with marketing business.

1Kotler, Keller, *Marketing Management, 13th ed., New Jersey: Pearson, 2009.*
2Company Profile, *About Rubbermaid Commercial Products, LLC,*
http://www.rubbermaidcommercial.com/rcp/company/.

A company's positioning and differentiation strategy must change as the product, market, and competitors change over the product life cycle. To say that a product has a life cycle is assert four things. What are those four things?

Product life cycle (PLC) is the individual stages of a certain product for which there will be period of stages on how it is develop, first introduce, grow, mature, and until phase out in the market. Product life cycle helps to determine the progression of a product which changes its impact in the marketplace in every different stage. Good positioning and differentiation strategy must be change each stage in order the product will survive longer in the market. To determine if a product has a life cycle, they are four things to assert in this subject as explain on the following paragraphs. These are: products have a limited life; product sales pass through distinct stages, each posing a different challenges, opportunities, and problems to the seller; profits rise and fall at different stages of the product life cycle; and products require different marketing, financial, manufacturing, purchasing, and human resource strategies in each life-cycle stage.

Products have a limited life. The life span of a certain product is depends on the set of period of each stages where it fluctuates the ratio of demand in the market. Every product has period of life in which some enjoyed a long or extended maturity stage while other products have short life or even don't reach its maturity stage. Technical products such as camera, cell phone or PC tablets are some of the examples that have limited life cycles. Normally, these products become obsolete like a PC tablet called Dell Streak 7 which was launched in 2010 but discontinued its production in 2011. The reason why product has a limited life is because once a product has been introduced and begins to roll out in the market, a competition starts that produce a better and a more advance technology for a similar product, or customer switches to another product or simply change their preferences. A product or service might be a success for a while but the demand in the market will certainly decrease eventually. In this case, the production and distribution of the product decline which force the company in deciding either to discontinue or withdrawn the product from the market or make some product modification to extend the product's maturity stage.

Secondly, product sales pass through distinct stages, each posing a different challenges, opportunities, and problems to the seller. Product life cycle involves performing different marketing strategies techniques as the market situation changes in every stage. In these periods, the seller may face a lot of challenges and problems how to sustain level of interest of the customers in the market, the same as how to maintain the competition on the similar product. This is true in the case of Hyundai Motors when they launched their first car in United States in 1986 which did not last because of series of cost cut backs that resulted to car severe quality problems and quality control issues Product sales dropped and profits went for repairing cars. But instantly, the company furnished a research on design, quality control and better manufacturing process. Afterwards, they have followed it by a media campaign and promotional offers to gain back their customers. Though it took years for them to retain their reputation, the company was successful to resolve their problem and fortunate to get back in competition. Since then, the company has produce high-quality and more new car models which earn a high profit level and increase sales volume each year.

Thirdly, profits rise and fall at different stages of the product life cycle. Product life cycle will have phases of profit of sales volume as the product moves its life through a cycle. Usually, a product that has just introduced has a low sales and negative profits because of a lower based price for the product. At this stage, a company is not concern about the profit level yet, even though the related cost and expenditure for production of a product is relatively high. Their first priority is to increase the awareness of the customer about the product, position it in the right target to the market and to have distinctive offers to defeat its competitors. Eventually, the sales and profits will rapidly increase during its growth, depending on demand from the market place until it will reach its maturity where the sales and profits will either be continuously increasing or decreasing.

The last thing to assert in product life-cycle is it requires different marketing, financial, manufacturing, purchasing, and human resource strategies in each life cycle stage. Every new product or service developed and launched in the market must go through stages of life cycle-introduction, growth, maturity, and decline. For this reason, each of these stages has distinct phases in terms of customer needs, company's goals, or type of competition in the market. As the product changes from one stage to another, various areas of management perform different marketing skills and techniques in order to increase the level performance of the product especially if there's a problem or challenges needed to use with respect in achieving profit potential on a desired level or any other related issues. In addition, marketing mix strategy is best to develop that expand segment of the product which consist of 4 P's -product, pricing, promotion and place in order to adjust the developing opportunities on the condition of each stages . All these business aspects that change in every stages of the product is based on the duration on how the product or services has been offered in the market which as mentioned that it requires alternative strategies in each areas of management activities.

The concept of product life cycle is a useful tool that guide marketers to understand the market dynamics of the product or service in each stages of life cycle which requires a great deal of marketing strategies to make right decision on introducing a product in the market. Furthermore, it will help marketing managers to plan ahead of what appropriate strategic marketing decisions are necessary in order to prepare them in handling any challenges that might face in the future. Finally, the nature of how differentiation and positioning the product to keep ahead from competition is not only important factor but it is required for conducting strategies for the success of the product.

---

[1]Kotler, Keller, *Marketing Management,* 13th ed., New Jersey: Pearson, 2009.
[2]Rob Wagner, *Hyundai Car History,* http://www.ehow.com/about_5243229_history-hyundai-cars.htm.

Various Factors have contributed to the increased importance of packaging as a marketing tool. List and briefly describe these events.

Packaging defines as activities for a process of designing and production of packages to protect the product for distribution or storage. In the old days, packaging was not been an important factor in marketing strategy. Mainly, the primary aim at that time in packaging was to protect the products from distribution, shipping and handling. The design of its package was an option and left out to save cost expenses incurred in packaging. But at present time, packaging becomes an element of a product strategy to generate sales and promoting to attract customer to buy the product. As we see hundreds of new products in the store, the first hand to beat the competition is to lure the customer on how the product looks on their package. First impression on the package is important in the eyes of the customer because it may accomplish the attraction of the product for them to buy it or at least help the purchasing decision for that matter. As a marketing tool, the increasing application of packaging has contributed various factors. These factors are as follows: self service; consumer affluence; company and brand image; and innovation opportunity.

The first factor is self service. At present, most of the products are place in the shelves especially in grocery items which are sold on a self-service basis. Every day, thousands of new products are out and introduce while some of them are just updated in a new package. If the product that customers use to buy has changed the package, the company has to develop a better one that is easier to recognize and visible in the eyes of the customer especially to those who are not familiar with the product. You do not want your shopper confuse on what they are seeing in the shelves and ask, is this the brand that I use to buy? Items like in grocery stores are one of those that look the same like chew bars and cereals for example. In order to look attractive, distinctive and get attention to the shoppers, the package should create contrast to the other products. It will help if you cite a question like, what you require to have an effective packaging that will contribute immediate impact on sales. As a shopper when I am looking for something and I do not know which one of the product that I will buy, I have things considering helping me on my purchasing decision. The favorable look of the package is necessary to achieve the goal to entice customer's interest in the product. It might be the attraction of the shape, color or design of the box. I also like reading the package box especially when it is a food item where I can find good information about nutritional health facts. So whatever phrase or message you can include is a big advantage. For me, it is not just a box or container; it is a box that is trying to communicate with me.

The second factor is consumer affluence. Shoppers are willing to pay more for an added value of the product which is normally considering its design and appearance, as well as the quality of convenience for ease of use. For instance, when I buy cookies I prefer the one with canister container. So after it is being emptied, it is still useful to keep other food product as a storage box. Some shoppers love to collect. For example, they prefer to buy perfume with decorative bottles so they can display it at home once it is emptied. When it comes to a food grocery item like frozen dinner, some or many prefers in a paper box that is easy to open which believe for healthy reasons is safer to heat it up in a microwave than a plastic. These days, companies produce packaging of their products for economic need of environment in which eco-conscious consumer's supports it highly. For whatever purpose or specific reasons, shoppers are ready to pay extra cost for additional benefits.

The third factor is company and brand image. Packaging is very important in every business because it is not only for product protection but it represents the brand image of a product in the market and identity of a company. Through great packaging, you can differentiate the brand of products from other competitors that will help the consumers what products they are intend to buy. With an increasing competition of brand products, packaging became a significant business tool in promoting a product. Nowadays, marketers develop a packaging with a distinct color or shape and with proper product information to identify the brand that is meaningful and more appealing to the consumer needs in which it can give a good first impression. For example, packaging box of product called Ipod from Apple, they may have simple color and shape design but it promotes its brand image of quality. The simplicity of their package box and yet creative and communicative makes it great which fulfills the purpose of good packaging from what the product is, good information, convenience, and that support their brand image. As a consumer, this was my purchasing experience when I bought this product for the first time.

Package innovation is the last factor to be considered that have contributed to the importance in packaging. This is important in every company that will bring new improved and better ideas in presenting the product to the consumers in which it will have the opportunity to have increasing benefits to produce a good profit. In recent years, packaging has increasingly developed and recognized by many of the marketers in order to promote their product. Package development which has a better feature and good quality material become more favorable in the eyes of the consumer that will support to create a better brand. This is the chance of every company to find a maximum value of sales revenue and get a long life value of their customers.

As a marketing tool, packaging play an important and significant role in the success of every product because this is the point of purchasing decision that will set in the mind of a consumer why you have to buy the product. It is substantial for marketers to consider objectives on how to introduce their product through effective packaging from design, ease of use, convenience, product information, and evidence of the brand sales in which it will also reflect the value of marketing mix: product, price, place, and promotion. As I mentioned, it is not just a box; it is a box that needs to convey a message about the product which will stick in the memory of every consumer.

Kotler, Keller, <u>Marketing Management,</u> 13th ed., New Jersey: Pearson, 2009.

In designing and evaluating an ad campaign, it is important to distinguish the message strategy or positioning of an ad from creative strategy. To develop a message strategy, advertisers go through three steps. List and explain these three steps.

According from previous chapters of Kotler's book, a customer buys products because of awareness of the importance and value of a product. Ad campaign is one to achieve this purpose which includes how to position a product. In message strategy, it is a process of ability to create a statement about the benefits of the product for a distinct group of audience. On the contrary as discussed in Chapter 17, creative strategy is how the marketers translate the statement that has been developed or content of message into an advertisement to a particular group of audience. In order to have an effective ad campaign, it is important to develop a message strategy. There are three steps that an advertiser follows to attain this goal. These are: message generation and evaluation; creative development and execution; and social-responsibility review.

The first step to develop a message strategy in an ad campaign is to create general statement on how to communicate to the target consumers which started by determining customer benefits that can be apply in advertising appeals. An advertiser should develop an impressive creative concept that will generate positioning of an ad into existence in a distinctive and persuasive way which can be as visuals, phrase or both. In order to determine the appeal that works for the target consumer and its satisfaction needs over products of the competitors, the advertisers should conduct market research to enhance the positioning of the brand that will meet objectives, build up the identity brand, and can relate to the audience. Then, the advertisers should create an ad theme. Advertising cost is relatively expensive so it can be useful to use strategy called open source or crowd sourcing in creating a theme. In this matter, the consumer acts as a creative team to get ideas on how to position an ad. This is an advantage for advertisers because not only it can save expenses from labor and research cost but it can also improve the creativity and productivity of advertising. As cited in the textbook for instance, Chevy invited customer to create ads in 2007 Chevy Tahoe SUV. However, this technique can also be a failure because since they are not employees, the executives can not demand and control them.

After evaluating and generating the message, it is time to bring the message to action into a motivating and memorable execution that will grab the attention of the target audience. This is the time that you can apply the creativity of the concept in translating the message. As much it is important what the message is, it is significant how to carry out this message to the audience through channels of media such as television, print, and radio ad which it can be more or less favorable depending on the area and what type of product or service where it will be sold. The following are some of the advantages and disadvantages of each advertising medium.

- **Television Ads** Television is the leading type of medium which allows to reach a wider audience locally or nationwide. It has the capacity to convey the message better with audio and visual but it can be costly because of its production and creation of the ads

- **Print Ads** Print media is based on newspaper and magazine which is popular medium to reach a group of target audience. Normally, it holds a good quality of the content of the ad while the cost is minimal. On the negative part, readers usually turn away the pages of the ads when reading either newspaper or magazine.

- **Radio Ads** This is a strong medium to reach specific audience segment which is flexible and relatively inexpensive. The target audience can listen the ads anytime or anywhere in the day. Because of visual images limitation, the impact of an ad can be less effective.

The last step is social-responsibility review. This is to address the legal and social issues that advertisers should not overlook in developing an ad campaign. There is a body of laws and regulations intended for the consumer to keep from being deceived or mislead by advertisers who has false claim, fraudulent advertisement or misrepresentation of a product. For instance, an advertiser makes exaggeration on the availability of a product, goods or services. To find out if it is true, consumer will buy the product. But, it will not really do the thing that they say in the ads. Or a certain company will advertise a discounted gift certificate. It means that you will pay a lesser amount on the actual price. Consumer like me sees that this is a great offer. One day to find out that when it is time to redeem it, the establishment do not recognize the gift certificate and refuse to accept it .

To be socially responsible in your ads, advertiser should not offend or make any racial remarks. Normally, advertisements are not just locally advertised but also nationwide. How you convey message in your product should also reflect in the cultural value of society or group of interest people. For instance, have you seen the commercial of "Burger King Texican Hamburger" with a short Mexican wrestler? It was an entertaining ad but many Mexicans were upset about it. For them, it showed that Mexicans are short and disrespectful for their flag used as an outfit. Advertisers should take consideration on the feeling of the minorities. They should be very careful and act on ethical standard on the ad campaign.

Advertising is one of the most effective marketing tools to attract customers and increase the awareness of the product which will reflect the brand differentiation key points and its value. While ad campaigns can be a success or failure, the three steps will guide the advertisers how to develop and create an effective ad campaign by learning what the product benefits, and how to inform, remind and persuade the target customer. Depending on the geographic area where the product is intended to be sold with a right message, I still believe that it can lead to a positive response from the target market.

Kotler, Keller, Marketing Management, 13th ed., New Jersey: Pearson, 2009.

ORGANIZATIONAL BEHAVIOR

Discuss the effects that corporate downsizing has had on the relationship between an organization and its members.

The concept of downsizing had taken place already long time ago. But it is just a few decades ago that many companies has to have corporate downsizing. They think that due to increasing competitive markets, globalization or some other economic changes such as evolution of new technologies, they are forced to do this process. It may involve using empowerment, contingent workers or outsourcing but by laying-off number of employees is the common process use by a company to reduce or cut back operating costs. In this stage, the fundamental changes in organizational behavior between the relationship of an organization and its member may have taken or resulted in various levels.

In 1990's, companies were downsizing as a management technique by cutting cost to maintain the productivity or profitability of a company and maximize its efficiency. This strategy maybe effective but it is indeed difficult because it will bring negative effect to the company particularly its employees. For example, my husband was terminated in his job at the Convention Center few years ago. He was let go because the company wanted to cut cost on payroll. The fact that he was the youngest and the newest employee; he was the first one to be laid off even if he was really doing a great job there. So while there is an emotional effect on his part after termination, the impact of downsizing among the employees who remains in the firm has more serious psychological effect. What are the negative consequences that the employees may experience after corporate downsizing? Often, they feel scared and worried that they might be the next one to be terminated. They feel depress and under severe stress because they have to manage extra workloads that the former worker usually does. They are also concern about how the management will treat them. In addition, they may experience to have a lower self-esteem and decrease their self confidence.

On the other hand, the relationship of the managers towards the surviving employees relatively changes also after the layoff. Oftentimes, they disconnect with their employees. Maybe, they feel guilty or blame about the termination especially when it is sudden. It can be disappointing to the remaining employees who became close friends to them and spent working for a long time and then suddenly leave. In this recession, it is only vital that the manager must start a strong commitment to the remaining employees to guarantee that their job satisfaction will stay favorable.

Another thing that affects the relationship between the company and its employees is the level of loyalty that they put on the company they are working. In the past, if you put all your hard work and loyalty on company where you work, you place your job more secured. For example, I am working with people who work more than a decade and almost spend their whole career in the organization. They have more job security even if they do not have new skills or higher education than those who are the newest employees. In our present society, this is no longer the case. Regardless of level education or loyalty in the company, you are not secured on your job anymore. As a result, the loyalty of the employees decreases because the company seems not to care the importance of this attitude on their company. After downsizing, the trust that the employees developed within the organization will might have to be re-establish all over again. Further, the feeling of remaining employees demoralized that they are becoming too anxious on their working status on the company. The relationship between the employer and the employee changes significantly due to these works- related behaviors and attitudes.

The work environment in the past is not the same in the present day where many employees realize that it is not enough to be loyal, hard worker or confident in order to keep the job but to assure that their skills and knowledge is up to date. For instance, even I think I have these qualities on my present job, I still continue to upgrade my skills and acquire other knowledge by taking up a higher education to have better job choices in the future. I try to learn different areas of work in the circuit court to be more useful if we are short handed of employees. I may or may not have a chance for job security but at least I am putting a good effort to make more flexible in any kind of work within an organization.

If the company is planning to have a corporate downsize, it can be at least avoided or reduce negative behavior in the remaining workers. In general, communication is always the key for good relationship between the employer and employee. Effective communication is very essential that will help the employees to understand the reasons and process of downsizing, In this case, the employees might become considerate on the company because they recognize themselves as part of the decision making. If an organization acknowledges the importance of the employees, both who are leaving and the remaining employees, it will bring a more positive effect on the relationship between employer and employee.

In conclusion, an organization challenges its effectiveness of human resource management about the corporate downsizing. As I mentioned, this is a difficult process which can be ineffective to fulfill its purpose why the company has to downsize. However, if this is done right with the proper planning, commitment and effective communication, it will make meaningful opportunities for developing new and motivation throughout the organization for achieving its overall goals.

George,Jones, Understanding and Managing: Organizational Behavior, 5ʰ ed., New Jersey: Pearson, 2008.

Discuss the four sources of self-efficacy identified by Albert Bandura.

The development of the social cognitive approach stress the significance of self-efficacy which refers to the perception of an individual on his capability to execute a certain task successfully according to a given situation. In other words, self-efficacy depends on what the person thinks or choices to make in order to fulfill a particular activity. This behavior will strongly affect the boundary or increase of person's choice of job or task, how a person can break the barrier or reach a goal in a bad situation. According to Albert Bandura, they are four sources in which self-efficacy is identified and developed. These are: past performance, vicarious experience or observation of others, verbal persuasion, and an individual's reading of his or her internal physiological states.

Past performance is the first and foremost source of self-efficacy in which a person performs based on his or her previous performance. Through their personal experience in the past, it has influence to create same anticipation on the outcome of their achievement in any task. It means that your self-efficacy will be high if you accomplished successfully and it will be low if it is unfulfilled or a failure. It is simply like following a behavior pattern. For instance, when I would like to learn something, I have the belief that I will able to educate myself either online or in person. Due to my optimism, it drives me to perform a task favorably which strengthens my sense of self-efficacy. On the other hand, some person has less confidence to complete a related task if they failed previously. Normally, they are worried that they will not succeed. This challenge can reduce the strength of efficacy expectations or it can lower sense of self-efficacy.

The second source is **vicarious experience or observation of other.** A belief to succeed can also be obtained by observing somebody completing the job successfully. It will also encourage you to try to do the things that you are afraid of or fail before. For example, I remembered when my 7 years old niece was making a beaded jewelry. While watching her, I told to myself that I can also do it. If in a young age she can do such a good beaded jewelry, there is no reason why I cannot do it. I was inspired and made an effort to try this project which turned it out successfully because of her. The same when I started working on my present job, I learned my tasks through watching my colleague working since I did not have a job training. In some circumstances, observation may demonstrate relevance in a similar situation for a better result on the past failed experience for others. This is true because I have learned to overcome those failures by watching somebody performing it successfully.

Verbal persuasion is the third source of self-efficacy. This can be obtained from the people who think that you have the ability to succeed. When someone convinces that you can do a task, it helps to strengthen your belief to achieve a certain goal because it will boost your confidence to succeed. For instance, a friend of mine insisted that I can paint. I told her that I have no knowledge about it. But she was kept insisting that I can. One day, I started reading some tutorials about painting and watched how to paint online. In my surprise, I tried and turned the painting good for a first timer. This person believes on my skills so she asked me again that I can paint her a portrait. I am not really confident but her encouragement made me do it. Though it was certainly difficult, I painted her a portrait with determination and it was a success. In contrast, if somebody discourages or criticize a person that he or she cannot do a certain activity, this will weaken a person's efficacy expectation.

The last source of self-efficacy is **an individual's reading of his or her internal physiological states.** This is a source that can be obtained from an emotional reaction of a person in a given situation. It means that by determining her own emotional state of mind or any physical reactions, a person can evaluate how positive she senses as she plans an activity. Let me give examples. When I was in high school, I got very nervous when I had to speak in front of the class. In this situation, I developed a weaker self-efficacy that I ended up not speaking at all. Through this experience, I have learned how to reduce stress and build my state of mind when I am in this challenging moment where I got better self-efficacy in the front of people. Also in the past when I was under pressure to finish the job completely, I was rushing my work so I could finish it. However, the level of my performance was less efficient because I felt stress and tense. I realized that the result of my work will be better if I am calmer and try to slow down.

Self-efficacy plays a significant part in every aspect of human life. A person's self reflection greatly influence on how to motivate and perform a particular activity. So if a person has a high sense of self-efficacy, he sees difficult task as a challenge, especially if somebody criticize his work. He can regain his confidence and try to succeed if he failed before. Moreover, he can develop further interest to do other activities and establish a strong commitment on doing it. On the other hand, a person with weaker sense of self-efficacy has a low confidence in achieving a goal. Usually, he remains on the failure of his experience rather than how to succeed. He prevents challenges to perform a difficult job. If he does, he will be under stress that can lead him to a poor result.

In conclusion, self-efficacy has an effective outcome on learning and performance because of its belief of capability to learn and accomplish a task successfully as it develops throughout the phase of life of an individual. In reality, it is not simple to sustain self-efficacy. Nevertheless, it is essential that a person must have it to maintain their determination and perseverance to succeed.

George,Jones, Understanding and Managing: Organizational Behavior, 5ʰ ed., New Jersey: Pearson, 2008.

Identify and review three major sources of interpersonal and intergroup conflict.

While an organization expected to work together, conflict may occur in which disagreement and interference arises from an individual or group within an organization for achieving a common values, goal or decision making. In the past, the outcome of organizational conflict always considered bad because it is normally resulted to decline the performance in the organization. However, conflict these days considered as a challenge and shows as an opportunity for productive change if it is carefully dealt and controlled by the management. They are three major sources of interpersonal and intergroup conflict where manager should acknowledge and seek for solution. These are: differentiation, task relationship, and scarcity of resources.

The first source of organizational conflict is **differentiation.** This is when the level of an organization is divided and its duties are grouped in different functions and department for completing a product or rendering a service. These differences can be resulted to conflict among the employees and its organizational units because of the following reasons:

- Difference in functional orientation. Employees have different tasks in their work unit and departments have different functions and goals. Therefore, it is hard for an organization to come to an agreement regarding the change they need in its organizational performance because one department may not agree with those of another. In my workplace for example, we prepare and file same style of summons, orders and other pleadings for each new or reopen cases. Though we work together, each division has a method of processing it. So if somebody asks our assistance on their paperwork which is not in our division and do it differently, the result can lead to a conflict.

- Status inconsistence. In an organization, if a certain group or working unit tries to promote their work, it can be a conflict because the other group may think that they have a better position in an organization, So if they started to perform any modification to achieve their goal, this may fail the goal of a related group.

Another source of organization conflict is **task relationship** in which conflict creates between an individual and group within an organization where the relationship of their tasks depend or link to one another. The following factors may develop conflict among them:

- Overlapping authority. This conflict happens when a manager in a different unit claim control in a company for the same activity. This means that a manager use the power to demand tasks to the employees while they have direct supervision of another manager. This is normally the reason why subordinates develop confusion whom will they follow first. In the textbook, it was cited that Gucci was battling who will control the company. Weinberg who was the new executive determined to bring his higher power over De Sole and Ford who were still in control on the company at that time. De Sole and Ford were in deep concern that it will hurt the organizational performance because Weinberg had no knowledge in fashion business. Their fight over power created conflict that resulted to a breakup.

- Task interpendencies. In a business, it is necessary to learn the role and responsibility of an individual or group to each other within an organization because the performance of one team can highly affect the performance of the other team. This is the reason that it is important to have good communication between groups or teams so they will be well coordinated with their activity. For instance, manufacturing business have different functions in completing a product so if one did not perform efficiently, the whole function will fail or suffer.

- Incompatible evaluation system. This is the way how an organization rewarded a team of any working units for their good performance in which conflict can occur among other groups. Moreover, it is difficult to assess performance when they have complicated relationship in their duties between groups that will create more conflict if rewarded. When I was still working at the theatre, the company was giving a reward for those who can up sell in the concession. I was working at the box office and sold a lot of tickets and with good customer reviews but I never been rewarded. It was fine for me but I am certain that somebody was not happy with that reward system.

Scarcity of resources is the last source of organizational conflict. If the organization has a limited resource; it will be allocated appropriately in various departments. In this case, competition among them who will get the better budget may exist. This happens often in any company. Our workplace for example, county office budgets are frequently the issue where conflict is present.

Interpersonal and intergroup conflict is a natural aspect and it cannot avoid in an organization. Nevertheless, conflict as I mentioned in the first paragraph is not all bad if it is well managed and effectively handled by the management. Furthermore, the power consume by any conflict can lead to positive results such as contributing to the production and profitability of the business which makes the organization successful. It is only essential that a manager should establish the ability necessary to manage and control it appropriately since it can result to the performance of the organization.

George, Jones, <u>Understanding and Managing: Organizational Behavior,</u> 5ʰ ed., New Jersey: Pearson, 2008.

Describe March and Simon's administrative model of decision making.

Decision making, a cognitive process of choosing an action in respond to solve a particular issue is one of the most significant activities in an organization that can bring a certain impact on the organizational structure of the company. The decision made by the management should be in the interest of the whole organization in which it will help to accomplish its objective and perform the duties efficiently. Effective decision depends on the type of approach that will be made in an organization. March and Simon's administrative model is one of the approach of decision making that I will discuss in the following paragraphs.

March and Simon's administrative model of decision making is a useful approach on how the organization reached an answer to the problem. I acknowledge that this model does not really consider a choice of best possible solution but consider the ones that are available which refers to satisficing. Oftentimes an organization faces more complicated issues so it is easier to find an acceptable solution that will work better in a problem and which can also help to resolve some other organizational issues rather than the optimal choice. With the availability of the chosen option, they will decide if it is sufficient enough for the problem. If the first choice did not work, another option can be tried until it will resolve the problem. To make it clearer, I would like to consider the things that characterize March and Simon's administrative model of decision making. These are satisficing, ethical decision making, and bounded rationality.

As I mentioned in the previous paragraph, satisficing demonstrates the searching of the acceptable and more realistic option until the sufficient answer to the problem is applicable. Simon and Mark indicated that because of lack of human mental behavior to be perfect; decision maker cannot determine the accuracy of appropriate possible effect of those alternatives. How the process of satisficing really works? For example, I suddenly need to make a beaded jewelry. I would need a jump ring to connect my beads to the clasp. The best size of jump ring for this project is 8mm with 1.3mm thickness. Since I just ordered this type of jump ring, I still have to wait a week or more to arrive this material. Instead of waiting which is a waste of time, I can use another size of jump ring. It may not be the best one but it is still good alternative to finish my project. If for some reason, it did not satisfy me on the first choice, I still have more options to choose from my other stuff until I find it satisfactory. In addition, satisficing can also occur when a group of people acknowledge the same answer to the problem. That is, they share a sound opinion as they analyze the significance of the facts available in certain situation.

The second consideration in a satisfactory decision making is to be ethical. This means that it should consider the impact of the decision which is acceptable to the majority as good where it will not damage its activities and members of an organization. The process of decision making is not simple because it is hard sometimes to evaluate whether the decision is considered to be ethical or unethical. Maybe is better to put a question like "What is the reasonable thing to do in this matter?" In this way, it will guide you on how to deal the situation ethically. So if you reached a decision, make a point to consider its impact and find out if it is a suitable decision. For instance, when somebody tries to give me a sort of tip for serving a good assistance, I always refuse to accept it and tell to the person that it is my job to offer our customer a satisfactory service. However, I appreciate the person acknowledged my good service. This standard ethical behavior is not only appropriate but it also creates a better business.

On the other hand, sometimes a person consciously chooses to make decision morally improper because it is an advantage on their part. And even if you seek to have ethical decision to settle an issue, you can still meet dilemma in your decision choices. Hence, it is difficult to make decision to be ethical and appropriate at the same time especially a situation that needs a response immediately because it can be challenging. Yet, it is essential to have it ethical in an organization where various issues in distinct level with numerous difficult choices should be given a careful consideration in seeking a satisfactory solution.

The last thing that characterize March and Simon's administrative model is bounded rationality. This indicates that the process of decision making has a limited performance in the amount of imperfect information available needed which is hard to search for an optimal solution particularly in a more complicated issues. Furthermore, there is also limit in the mind of human being to process this information where the decision made is based through logical thinking. In another words, a decision is just simply good enough to solve a problem. This is the reason that a decision maker is not fully aware what will be the outcome associated with the alternative.

In an organization, a manager has a responsibility to make a decision that is required to operate a business particularly if there is a situation needed to resolve. According to March and Simon's administrative model , it is not easy to find optimal solution to define the problem and issues face by the organization as described in classical model because of specific factors as mentioned that constrains to apply rational reasoning. For this reason, a manager chooses to decide the simplest and acceptable choice without any complicated reasoning in each alternative. Thus, an organization utilize this model on decision making is better to comprehend its outcome both bad or good that can be use in improving and learning experience in a business and which it can make you a better decision maker.

George, Jones, <u>Understanding and Managing: Organizational Behavior,</u> 5[h] ed., New Jersey: Pearson, 2008.

BUSINESS ETHICS

Business ethics typically involves five kinds of activities. Assess and detail each one.

When we say ethics, many would mean it is an individual's knowledge of what is good or bad using various distinct senses. In business, the decision to act morally in an organization is the right one. This would not only bring certainty to an organization but also enhance the image of an organization as a whole. However, a moral standard applied in business could also be applied to individual's daily lives such as stealing, cheating or lying. In simple words, business ethics is the set of laws of ethics that administer on how an organization or companies function, how decision determines and how the employees are taking care of. Acting in a moral way would tell you a course of action if it is "right" or "wrong". In this case, you have the choice to do what is right. They are common five types of activities in business ethics in which I am going to discuss.

1. **Application of general ethical standard in business practices or other specific cases**

   In this first activity, it is to determine if the course of action is morally or immorally acceptable. Moral awareness is a basic element of the business organization or any specific cases. For instance, you saw your manager taking home supplies of your office. This is not only ethical but he could also be a bad model to the workers. As an individual, we could ask ourselves what we have to do in some situation. Nevertheless, not all rules can expect all possible circumstances. In some cases, it will create problems and conflict within an organization. That is the reason that it needs a careful attention to the ethical rules and to analyze these rules if they are still beneficial to use during the changing economic and social circumstances. Nonetheless, business ethics does not only engage in applying moral standards but also to balance and to change in consideration of current facts, techniques to a more appropriate and acceptable practice.

2. Metaethical

This is the second activity in which involves analysis if the ethical language that is administered in any course of action of an individual can also be used for organization, companies or any business entities. Some of these practices might not be applicable to the standards of an organization. In meta ethics, it questioned how we comprehend, being knowledgeable and intending meaning when we talk ethical statements. I would say, for instance, "Stealing is ethically wrong." Metaethics is about the basic understanding of what I meant by this statement, "What did I mean to be ethically wrong"? The response to this question would have assumptions of ethical reasoning in determining the certainty of the arguments morally. But would it be applied by the theory of general ethics in which commonly involves in other areas in the life of an individual? There is a logical relation between ethics in business and in general. However, not all metaethical questions used in business ethics supported in theory generally.

3. Analysis of the presupposition of business

In this activity, part of it tries to examine the presupposition ethically and from the moral perspective. The function of the business is within the system where a country allocates resources, goods or services in a given society. For that reason, one of the appropriate tasks of business ethics is an effort to answer an inquiry regarding the morality in general and precise morality of economic system specifically in America. In this system, any course of action is subject to moral standards and examines the general moral principles and rules which increase the level of relevant questions by the usefulness of the moral terms to determine this system. Further, it needs to determine the business structure that develops moral responsibility and to find out what particular functions of an organization is necessary for development.

4. **Business ethics is sometimes directed by embedded problems to move beyond the field of ethics into other area of philosophy and into other domain of knowledge.**

This fourth activity is learning the established point of issues not covered the field of ethics into different parts of philosophy and a particular segment of expertise. This is significant in handling on macromoral issues with questions addressing moral issues of a company or society other than those limited to individual issues. In multinational companies, for example, there are always various distinct ethical issues due to cultural diversity that they have a distinct way of doing things in business from one country to another. In this case, it is common that they deal and settle a resolution to the problem and try to find out in what other aspect has to be the issue in business ethics. Accordingly, there will be a systematic examination of this problem to identify which one is ethical and non-ethical and to explain its language and the degree of moral statement. This responsibility at times has to do with diminishing the moral issues to organizational or any business related problems or the other way around.

5. **Describing morally praiseworthy and exemplary acts of a person in business or specific company.**

Generally, once you hear the word "business ethics", it is generally a reaction to unethical behavior in the business such as fraud, bribery or corruption. They are mostly brought into public interest in which it would circulate the information on by broadcasting, for instance, the Enron scandal. However, business ethics is not just about unfavorable task of attempting to explain what the activity is morally unacceptable, but also promoting a sense of achievement for admirable conduct by an individual such as the likes of Martin Luther King, Jr. or Mother Theresa who became the role model and inspiration of many lives. In the world of business, there are also moral ideals that we could see as an exemplary of doing good works that could be an inspiration for creating a goal in an organization. Similarly, it would achieve in conforming moral and professional behavior as well as judgment on the essential distinguishing character of a person.

In summary, ethics pertains to moral awareness of an individual with respect to actions either right or wrong. In business, however, the decisions of an organization are made by a group of individuals where they must choose what they believe is an ethical one in making decisions. It is true that if a company and its people act in a socially responsible way are more likely to appreciate the success of their business. The knowledge of the typical activities involved in business ethics is very useful in awareness for doing the right action, dealing with moral problems more appropriately and creates arguments demonstrating the business practice that is unethical. So whether the business is small or big or no matter what the degree of profitability of a company, business ethics provides significant key of longstanding success in an organization.

DeGeorge, Business Ethics, 7th ed., New Jersey, Pearson/Prentice Hall, 2010.

Determine and assess the actions required when applying moral reasoning.

Actions derived from the reflection on what we think and these actions could have an impact on others. In order to analyze if any course of action is right or wrong, there is a process that needs to be applied called moral reasoning. It is a way that applies a reasonable means of thinking of an individual or a group of an effort to carry out a right decision morally. In doing so, it is vital to acknowledge the significance and taking actions required in making a moral decision. However, before we could start this process, it is imperative the comprehension about moral reasoning and consider what approach is essential in an effective application of moral analysis. These approaches are ***deontology,*** a process that involves analysis of ethical actions and responsibility on the basis if either its action is appropriate or not under a set of laws and ***utilitarian,*** a process by which morality of an action is decided on the outcome of its action. In this paper, I will discuss this subject matter in the following paragraphs.

Some users of these approaches have their preference, using one or both, depending on a particular situation. There is no factual evidence that deontology is better than using utilitarian. Regardless of what to use, it is important to create a compelling and reasonable approach in making ethical decisions by following on the actions necessary when applying moral analysis. It is only necessary to use all possible methods and actions to support an argument. So what are these actions or process?

In solving an issue, the first thing to do is you have to find what the facts are. In order to examine the facts appropriately, it is vital to acquire and find out more detailed information relating to the subjects which only depend on what the moral issues are. However, if we could not come out with all applicable facts, we could identify some credible presumption on the facts that is overlooked.

When we gathered all the facts, it is time to identify what is the issue. We could start asking a question like, "Do the issue a violation of moral or organizational rules?" or "Is it dealing with an individual, a group or an organization?" Recognizing what the degree of the moral issue would make it easier to determine who will be involved and affected in making the decisions. It is also good to consider categorizing which ones are major, minor or least important ethical issues. Once the problem has been identified, we could proceed to find what ethical rules are to be adapted. In evaluating the issue, we should know if there is a relation to the situation under careful thought on the suitable rule. Sometimes, the problem could be not by a great extent resolved that we need to choose a different approach which is more precise and appropriate. For example, if a particular situation involves causing damage or harm but resulted to a positive outcome which justifies you from wrong doing, you might able to apply utilitarian. However, if it involves rights, duties or justice, we m

After careful considerations citing each case and finding out which more applicable approach, the solution carried out might have different direction. In this case, we could apply our moral imagination in all available options to solve the issue. That is applying our knowledge to reason properly with what must be done in a certain situation. Oftentimes, whatever method that has applied, it produces the same moral conclusion. Nevertheless, it is not the case all the time. If it happens, it is necessary to examine carefully the certainty and the efficiency of the analysis. Then, if the final decision still different, we could make a choice which argument is more powerful and easily understood in which it combines with a reasonable and productive manner with other ethical conclusions. Keep in mind that when dealing issues and conflicts in business, the ethical rules support the lowest level of moral behavior of an individual which is in conformity with the rules.

Finally, we completed the analysis and arrived at a decision after a careful thought. Then, we could challenge ourselves to reply these questions such as "Are we pleased with the conclusion?", "Is it reasonable with appropriate and sound judgment?" or "Would it be beneficial if we present it to others?" In some cases, it might have some situations that somebody might contradict on your decision. If this occurs, respond to their disagreement and demonstrate why your analysis is a better than all others. Or maybe if we found any error or mistake, we could just modify it.

In conclusion, the degree of beliefs about human behavior between right and wrong is significant in business ethics where moral reasoning affects the productivity of a company in the free or common market. I believe that regardless of what approach we choose, we should use our logical thinking in making an ethical decision with a set of actions required on the basis of persons affected and specific situation.

Moreover, moral reasoning should be done carefully in accordance with ethical principles and act with appropriate manner either applicable in business or in all areas of an individual's life. In some cases, we could have difficult and complicated issues. Therefore, it is only essential to follow these actions required in applying moral reasoning which would be very useful in achieving a conclusion accordingly and effectively.

DeGeorge, Business Ethics, 7th ed., New Jersey, Pearson/Prentice Hall, 2010.

Evaluate the concept of strict liability.

Every day, many buyers consume a product that they think are agreeable to their purchasing needs. However, a consumer might experience an injury or accident while using this product. In this incident, could we recover any damages occurred by using this product? Who we suppose to bring legal claim against with? In this essay, I will talk about the concept relating to the subject matter which is concept of strict liability.

When we purchase a product, we assume that we have chosen a right product based on its description. If the product did not meet with our expectation and we got hurt using this product, our dissatisfaction could lead a complaint with the manufacturer. In most cases, the producer included a warranty as an agreeable agreement with consideration to the merchandise or goods purchased when it breaks or damages it within certain of time. On the other hand, if the consumer incurred an injury using the product, the manufacturer could be accountable to pay damages. In this case, the consumer might file a claim based on strict liability. This means that the manufacturer is responsible for the harm done by the product regardless of whose to blame for the injury. This not the same from being careless or failure to take care of the product in which you experience harm. In recent cases of strict liability, the U.S. law permits granting the consumer to award damages to the physical injury and the other losses such as medical cost or loss of wages together with punitive damages. This additional cost is accomplished to penalize the manufacturers for having a product defectively that brings harm to the public and to prevent other similar actions of negligence that may occur.

Strict liability is a legal principle of law that holds an individual or a company accountable for the damages without proving the evidence of fault. This doctrine provides the public of safety to do harm or injury. Nevertheless, different opinions have been likely to show that the strict liability is either unjustifiable or unfavorable to business organizations. Let us review briefly these fundamental arguments which have three sections on the following paragraphs.

First, strict liability is defended by the principle of "deep pocket". When an injury or accident happens, who should be the acceptable position to shoulder the damages? Although, we could say that the producer of the product is the responsible one to pay the cost, this might not be accurate. However, these type of individuals or organizations are mostly wealthy and resourceful. They are certainly worth to bring legal lawsuits against with. It is likely that the plaintiffs would target to sue them or look for more resources. For example, instead suing the distributor of the product, suing a manufacturer or both would be much better. In this case, corporation or any business entities should have liability insurance in order to cover the damages to the lawsuit if it occurs. In addition, it would be advantageous to include a value added cost of insurance against its product's price.

Secondly, strict liability supplies a desired effect and a needed motivation to manufacturers in building their product more t free from harm. For this reason, it is likely that they might be accountable for any harm that could happen using their product; it is significant to develop a better product that is moderately safe. Normally, before the products distributed out in the market, they run a test and assure that they are no risk while using it. It is known that some products have danger while using it. Some of these are electronics, cleaning supplies, drugs or chemical spray products. In order to avoid misuse or injuring someone, the manufacturer included an added feature such as warning label or safety instruction to protect the consumers from being harm and to inform them for possible cautions.

The final argument with strict liability is that when the product found to have some defect, they should correct the issue as soon as possible or recall the product due to safety concern so that it would avoid more future damages. Further, the injury caused by this product of the common course of use could be properly compensated.

Certainly, not all individual who hurt using a certain product could bring a strict liability case. It is not just because you were injured, you could file a lawsuit already. In order for a consumer to do this, it must have been proven that the product is defective or it did not function based on it standard use. Further, if you have misused the product, you could not either bring it to the court. For example, you purchase a medicine and it is strictly warned you that you have the dosages of use as a warning. Yet, you still took those medicines more than the dosage where you got the overdose. In this case, the product did not cause the damage because it is common knowledge that if you get an overdose, the harm would certainly occur.

Liability with a product is not just a moral issue that you resolved. This is something that a producer of a product has a moral obligation to make it free from harm or risk of use. If these products are dangerous, the producer should be properly informing the consumers of possible harm could happen if they misuse it. If the manufacturer deliberately ignores the safety of the consumer, making false statement of the product, creating unsafe products or not informing the public about the risk, these are considered to be immoral and improper actions of any business organizations. In spite of, strict liability is the legal principle of supporting to develop and increase security and assurance with the products.

In today's competitive market, it is without a doubt that adding safety element for their products might not be able to compete successfully with other manufacturers. This could be true if the consumers are not ready to pay more for this product's added feature. Normally, they are just putting their trust in the product they bought. So it is uncertain if the companies have an ethical obligation to make products that are free from danger. Regardless, I still strongly believe that it is reasonable to do what is morally correct which is to be truthful with the customers especially when dealing on the best interest of them. If not, they might regret it later. That is the reason that there is strict liability to protect the well-being of the society for getting harm or injured.

DeGeorge, Business Ethics, 7th ed., New Jersey, Pearson/Prentice Hall, 2010.

Compare such terms as facts, knowledge, understanding, information and data.

When we speak about words such as facts, knowledge, understanding, information and data, what comes to our mind is computer, an electronic device that becomes vital in processing information. This is where the people gave so much attention that these groups of words are often used in the kind of activities on a day to day basis. Usually, these terms are repeatedly used in the place of each other in the common language. There is a general difficulty in understanding on these terms. Although, they have the similar idea, they have fundamental distinctions of their meanings. Numerous persons expressed a different opinion thoroughly about an explanation of the meaning each of these terms. In order to understand how each of these words complements and distinct to each other, we will analyze these terms in accordance with their meaning and purpose in a different view. So let us start to analyze these terms with a more detailed description.

1. **Facts** are fragments of information on a situation that has happened. It signifies the correctness or validity of certain information or statement which is usually supported by gathering evidence. For instance, the phrase "In fact" this gives you the certainty of the word that is true. It is sometimes entered in a processing machine as the data onto relational database. Also, this term is connected with knowledge and information as they immeasurably complement each other which is normally applied accomplishing in making certain decisions. For example, if there

are large numbers of facts blended and combined as knowledge, then the facts could turn to be knowledge too.

2. **Data** is raw facts that have been gathered and collected. It can be in the form of letters, numbers, word or characters. There is a common issue relating to data and facts because there is a time that data used as facts. This could only be possible as mentioned in the previous paragraph if it is in relational database. Yet, data does not have substance to other things and has no benefits further itself. For instance, a table of names: this is insignificant because it does not include what these names are for. Data will only be useful once it is processed in some manner called information which gives substance for data. Further, a data could be own as a personal ownership in which has been stored in a processing machine and the owner has the sole control over it. This means that the data could be erased or edited.

3. **Information** is a compilation of data that includes appropriate meaning. You could move or control the data using a program that a human could understand better. The substance of these data becomes information. In general, it can be used to acquire a more relevant implication of patterns. The aim at information is to help in making decision or resolving an issue. However, this "meaning" might not inevitably be valuable. For instance, the data collected in a database could create as information because these data have relevant connection with other data. On the other hand, information could turn to a fact if the data could provide evidence for it.

4. **Knowledge** is a collection of facts or information that is obtained through learning or experience. It derives from the information along with information obtain from the data. Knowledge is seemed to be the most profound and valuable in contrast with data and information. However, it is true that you could not acquire knowledge without information. In order to obtain knowledge, it is essential that you have some logical and intellectual ability while it is not needed with information.

5. **Understanding** is the ability to interpret a certain subject matter or situation. Understanding is not the same as in knowledge although; it is actually consisted of it. It is because that understanding requires a deep level of thinking skill than just knowing something. For example, an individual may have a careful study in a particular course but it might not develop an effect on the highest degree or memorizing a poem without understanding the content of it. On the other hand, it is true that they complement each other and both of them are essential.

Let us summarize these terms with a simple illustration.

TERM	EXAMPLE	ANSWER TO QUESTION	CONSIST OF	EXPLANATION
Data	I have one appliance.	—	Raw	It shows one.
Information	This appliance is a refrigerator.	What	Data	Now, we know what is an appliance and its features.

Knowledge	Refrigerator is used for purpose of storing the foods to keep cool and fresh.	How	Information	We can identify the pattern and put into use of it. This is a true statement that could be a fact.
Understan-ding	The food should be stored correctly in a refrigerator and put it with the right cooling temperature to avoid development of bacteria.	Why	Knowledge	There is a fundamental, general standard comprehension that carries out the appliance's function. This is true so we could say it is a fact too.

In conclusion, these terms are components in the process with the world of computing or human way of thinking. Although each of these terms has a distinct purpose and meaning, they are associated with each other that they could not be completed without the need of the other term. For this reason, knowing their relationship and differences could make us better understand the sequence of the learning process from these terms in which we can apply it in our daily lives in making a decision and activities in life.

DeGeorge, <u>Business Ethics</u>, 7th ed., New Jersey, Pearson/Prentice Hall, 2010.

LEADERSHIP

List and define the leadership theory paradigms.

Leadership is a subject that creates enthusiasm and significance in the success of a profession or an organization since back during the old days. We could ask ourselves, what made leaders like Martin Luther King or Mother Theresa became so influential that their style was effective to many who followed them? Was it because on the type of situation that they were leading to? Or it was because they had good traits? To answer these questions, I will talk about the theories about leadership paradigm and describe its basis of the process of leading a group or an organization.

First, let me point out what is leadership theory. It is a statement of opinion of features of leadership that the theories have useful importance for better comprehension and the capacity to be an effective leader. The leadership theory is categorized by four main classifications. These are: trait, behavioral, contingency and integrative. With these classifications, we could explore how these outstanding leaders are made. A leadership paradigm is a common approach to build an understanding and develop a method of researching about the leadership. But during the 60 years times, these leadership theories have shifted to innovative idea of leadership: from the management to the leadership theory paradigm.

The Trait Theory Paradigm

Early research in leadership was explained that the success of leadership depending on an individual that was born in set of related traits. These traits or qualities such as self-confidence, determination, intelligent, persuasiveness and other physical and psychological traits examined by the researchers which recognize them to become a good leader. In early 1930's and during 1940's, researchers administered studies of various traits. Nonetheless, nobody has come up with the entire record of these traits that will assure a leader to become successful in leadership.

The Behavioral Leadership Theory Paradigm

In the year of 1950's, studies shift its paradigm from trait theory to give attention on the distinguishing style of a leader or describe what they actually do in numerous situations. The common example of this theory is Mintzberg's ten managerial roles which are the basis of a manager or member job descriptions. Like in trait theory, there was no compliance with behavioral theory that these styles can make you an effective leader in any situations. Nevertheless, they have developed two universal measures, task-oriented which aim is to finish the job accordingly and people-oriented which aim is to create friendly atmosphere at work. Applying both of these measures has significance of fulfilling leadership success suitable for the needs of the management to a particular situation.

The Contingency Leadership Theory Paradigm

In 1960's, the effort of the researchers to discover the best style in both the trait and behavioral leadership theory has become evident that there is no best style in leadership in all circumstances. Therefore, they use these theories as a basis to decide the most suitable style in leadership. This is how its paradigm shifts to the contingency leadership theory. It describes that the favorable outcome of leadership is based on the good traits of a leader and the characteristics of a follower in the appropriate settings.

The Integrative Leadership Theory Paradigm

In the year 1970's, the trait, behavioral and contingency leadership theory was not working in finding the best approach in effective leadership and the paradigm started to switch to the integrative leadership theory. Hence, theories of integrative leadership made an effort to integrate the three previous leadership theories to demonstrate the understanding and the quality of traits and behaviors of the leaders by their followers that develops a relationship to achieve a common goal. The theories investigate why the same characteristics of a leader might have a distinctive outcome of their followers. As a result, it grants the leader to establish creatively and become more adjusted to a certain situation.

From the Management to the Leadership Theory Paradigm

Over the decades, the pursuit of researchers on the old leadership paradigms does not fulfill in the current global economy. A leadership plays a significant role in an organization. In our present days, a manager should only not know how to manage but also must have the ability to lead, establish and understand the skills to tackle a task by inspiring others. A leader and its members agreed a goal together and motivate each other to achieve a common goal for the success of an organization. In this case, the traditional management styles shift from the management to the leadership theory paradigm. Although, there is distinction between a manager and a leader, it can be both performed as one effectively. However, there is an overlap between two paradigms that is, a managers and leaders should be together in an organization to become successful.

The distinctions of these leadership theories in which researchers have been suggested and studied over the decades are just one-dimensional. As a matter of fact, these theories are adapted to different forms of the same circumstances or experiences. Although, I believe that shifting to management to the leadership theory could have a more positive outcome approach to leadership, a leader should apply all the basic leadership theories and takes the good qualities of each one and use them when the situation calls for. It is only to remember that it involves a leader, followers, and the situation which it could be easier about an individual to learn and encourage the complicated subject of leadership.

Lussier and Achua, Leadership: Theory, Application, & Skill Development, 5th ed., Boston, Cengage Learning, 2013.

Explain the differences between position and personal power.

As mentioned in Chapter 3 of the textbook, leadership is about motivating others to accomplish organizational goals. That is, both a leader and a follower must motivate each other. Influencing is the core element of leadership. Although, you may bring power even you are not a leader, you cannot be one if you are lacking in it which it is the basis of certain characteristics and abilities. While the application of power in an organization is significant, it is necessary to distinguish what type of power to be applied to develop a powerful relationship between the leader and his followers. These powers are categorized into two sources which I am about to discuss how these two powers differ from each other on the following paragraphs. These are position and personal power.

Position power

This power is acquired through a title or position in an organization. It means that you have the authority to lead and make choices of how to do it. It is an obligation to incur best outcomes of the team that should not be neglected. When you are in position, you have the power asking your people what to do. You would find that there is usually a manipulation of action rather than influencing. For example, I am the manager or owner of a firm. I could say, "I could terminate you if you do not perform your duties accordingly."In this case, I am using my title to exert power to them. Nevertheless, using power in an organization should look at in an advantageous way. A manager uses this power to accomplish their goal which is the capability to reach its purpose and finish whatever tasks needs to be done. I remembered back in the days when I was teaching in accounting. It is significant that the students should listen and follow instructions if they wanted to get better grades. I used this position to do their assignment and study hard to reach an agreeable outcome of their studies.

An individual using position power to get what they want from their followers is usually no sense of influencing. Although they are leading a group or organization, some of them do not make them a leader particularly if you throw your title at them. Further, they are usually only doing their tasks for the reason that it is their job description and their subordinates would be frightened to get fired if they do not perform their tasks properly. As a result, leader and its members do not have harmonious relationship.

Personal Power

This source of power is different from position. It is the power acquired from within an individual on the basis of special talents and abilities to motivate others without a title or position in an organization. When an individual is using personal power, his followers have the freedom whether to go along or not what a leader wants them to do. Unlike in position power, they have no option but do whatever their leader tells them to do. Personal power is like in charismatic leadership where a leader encourages their followers to achieve a common goal. If you are a leader of a group, you encourage them to do things in a way to accept you in order to achieve a goal. In this power, some of their followers have influence over their leaders too. For example, a follower could say, "I am going to do what he says because he is an expert at that subject and I will do it the way he suggested. Besides, he appreciates me." Unlike in position power, a manager or a leader just uses his position to influence them.

Although, it is understood that to some consideration of a leader who has a position as a "boss" have also confidence using personal power where they could maintain their ability to reach the goal by influencing and persuading them. Through personal power, a leader and followers could build a good relationship and bring the best of them as a leader and as a follower. In addition, if you engage in personal power, you could create a greater support and commitment and trust from the followers than the one in position power.

In conclusion, leading is the major managerial task in an organization. Therefore, a manager should be a leader. However, it is a fact that not all of them are said to be leaders. Moreover in the current world of business competition, managers should acquire powerful leadership traits that will make him a successful leader. It is something to have a quality how to influence and inspire others and make yourself being a role model for your subordinate to follow you. In this case, the employee's motivation, quality of their work and their decision would be balance. Consequently, it is better for a manager to exercise both position and personal power by using it properly to have success in the outcome of any business or an organization.

Lussier and Achua, <u>Leadership: Theory, Application, & Skill Development</u>, 5th ed., Boston, Cengage Learning, 2013.

Distinguish between charismatic and transformational leadership.

Considering that a leadership approach might be important aspect in achieving a success in a business, researchers have examined and determined various styles with variable outcomes of a particular organization. Two of these leadership styles are charismatic and transformational. These leadership styles might have similarities on the basis of its fundamentals, collection of qualities or the effects of their leader's behaviors to their followers. Some researches make no differentiation between charismatic and transformational because they thought they are alike and one especially they both possess charisma. Nevertheless, they are significantly distinct and therefore described as two separate approaches to leadership. In this essay, I will discuss the areas that differentiate charismatic and transformational leadership on the following paragraphs.

The focal point in both charismatic and transformations are as regards to change. It is true that both of these leadership styles could bring a vision and create a powerful connection with the followers by using the charisma. However, some transformational leaders do not have charm, appeal or lacking charisma. Notwithstanding, they can still come up with a change in an organization of a very satisfactory result without the effect of charismatic nature. You see, charisma is the key component in follower perception in charismatic leadership while it is only one of the attributes of a transformational leader. It is not its defining attributes in transformational leadership. In spite of charismatic leadership's charm, its leaders may not want to change anything because they are more worried about themselves than others. In contrast, a transformational leader challenges status quo and draw more concern on his followers. One of the most current examples is the Facebook Founder named Mark Zuckerburg. Despite the fact that he is a successful and attained outstanding transforming an outcome of social media, he is a shy and quiet person. Certainly, he is not type of a leader who is charismatic.

Secondly, another difference lies on how the charisma or transformer achieves its label. Because charisma is a compelling quality that can inspire commitment and loyalty in others, a follower in charismatic leadership develops attribution on their leader as an exceptional quality of leadership. In short, followers look up the leader as a role model. This followers' perception of the leader's attitude, ability and viewpoint of the situation will make them more motivated to achieve their goal. In transformational leadership, the leaders are described on the basis of previous evaluation of their achievements instead of its members' attribution on their leader. The leader aims for a change by motivating and inspiring his subordinate for a fresh vision and opportunities. Bill Gates is one of these leaders that transformed our community to make life easier about innovation in the world of computers.

The third distinction is regarding the mind-set of its leader. Normally, charismatic leader inclined to achieve a goal through political and social change way of thinking. That is, they oppose to do something such as fighting on status quo. Charismatic leader has a powerful self-belief and high confidence regarding the vision and approach for which he is leading to. Because of this inmost belief and confidence, a leader takes a greater risk of pursuing an effort to achieve the objective which is usually resulted from an agreeable outcome. On the other hand, transformational leadership is more strategic way. That is, its leader is setting a precise planning in accomplishing a certain goal on a long term basis. Unlike in charismatic leadership, transformational leadership is often facing up the status quo and do not have fear of disappointments. The leader and its members work together for whatever problem they may face or fulfilling of their visions. They are on a mission for an agreeable change and regulate the strengths and flaws in an organization with arising favorable circumstances and threats.

What career path that each leadership type is likely to follow is another area of difference. In transformational leadership, both the leader and its members involve in transformation process where they motivate and encourage each other. The leader puts assumptions of his followers that they have vision. And so the leader motivated them with eagerness and energy as they could contribute to express their ideas clearly on this vision in the fulfillment of their objectives. Further, the leader acknowledges its members of the problems and inspires to resolve this problem with the best of their ability. As a result, it will not only promote the strength of their team work but also to show followers' qualities as a transforming leader and not just an individual. On the contrary, a charismatic leader likes to take a risk and convince others to do so. Their strong belief and great self-confidence leads them to pursue something particularly at the time of crisis which is frequently resulted to a positive outcome. This is the reason why their followers have faith with their abilities and skill to lead them during state of emergency. They see their leader as their hero on a certain situation.

Another difference is about how its leader perceives their personal meaning or purpose in life. As a charismatic supporter, it is by faith and spirituality that stimulate them to have personal meaning and purpose for a better life. This is the same in charismatic leader that faces struggles and challenges leading mission of transformation and makes their vision meaningful. It is the key element of motivation that this leader battles with well-being of his follower and for a better society or an organization. Do you think that a transformation leader has this belief? The important thing in transformational leadership is assuming responsibility for the circumstances on bringing a clear perception of the team's objectives and performs the work appropriately. A transformational leader might want to be a CEO of an organization. However, I believed that the plan and setting of their shared vision of his subordinate provides meaning and purpose in the fulfillment of an organizational objective in a natural way.

Finally, although both charismatic and transformational leaders are risk-takers, charismatic emotional degree of resistance and issues is greater than in transformational. It is a fact that sometimes they put high risk of their life and not afraid if there is a great danger in fulfilling their vision. Look at civil right leader, Martin Luther King Jr. who received several death threats on the time of his movement. This did not stop him believing his vision until he was assassinated. In transformational leadership, the leaders know when there is a greater risk that they might face. In a business viewpoint, usually a transformational leader loses their title in an organization or fired them in their job. Moreover, a leader focuses on providing an authority as head of an organization and using this position to resolve issues in such a way its firm decision serves the company.

In summary, charismatic and transformational leadership are different in approaching their followers and the process of influencing them. Charismatic leader empowered by vision's submission of his follower and its fulfillment which depends on how the leader energizes them. Whereas in transformational leadership, there is a power sharing with vision, its achievement and the transformation process on the leader and its followers. These two leadership styles are both important in achieving an organizational goal in which it shows connection between the leader and its members that will fit in a particular situation.

Lussier and Achua, Leadership: Theory, Application, & Skill Development, 5th ed., Boston, Cengage Learning, 2013.

Describe the role of leadership in creating a learning organization.

The current economy, technology, globalization and market competition are changing tremendously. It only requires for an organization to challenge the status quo and upgrade the skills and knowledge to conform the present labor market. In this case, a learning organization has developed where a group of individuals are involved in a continuous learning on expansion of their abilities and skills to stay competitive in the modern world of business. This is the reason that the role of leadership plays a substantial part in developing a learning organization for which it is a key to motivate progress of it by accomplishing its business approach. In order to create a learning organization success, the leadership should be effective. The leadership's role is important to the success of a learning organization. The leaders are in charge in enhancing an organization while the members constantly developing their capacities for building the future. It requires the need of collective knowledge throughout the system that will lead to complete transformation. Researchers suggest that they are critical features that the leader must acquire in creating learning organization in which I am about to discuss on the following paragraphs.

Create a shared vision of the future

An organization is searching for a powerful ideal leader in order to maintain the growth and competitive benefits greater than others. As discussed in the previous chapters in the textbook, sharing a vision is vital in an organization. A leader should have the knowledge to motivate his members to take part the views of an organization along with his own vision and inspire them to work with it. In this way, a leader and its team has a shared comprehension on the vision and goals in learning organization in which it could develop the same interests and sense of common purpose of all levels of management activities. Further, it could promote the learning environment better in an organization.

Empowering and training followers to handle environmental challenges

I have learned from transformational leadership that a leader acknowledges problems with his followers and inspire them it the best of their ability to resolve it. Due to rising threats to the present business condition, a leader in a learning organization should improve the confidence

in the members to solve any problems and motivates them to take a risk reasonably. In this case, it could be an opportunity for any mistakes endured on the past to learn and acquire new ideas and provide a favorable circumstance for them to solve any future challenges and issues with organizational environment. As for me, this is how I have learned more through my flaws.

Modeling learning behavior

One of the best approaches of learning knowledge or abilities is modeling. In creating learning organization, the members would certainly want to know who they are supposed to follow or lead on how to do something. In this manner, it would grant to challenge them to inquire and gain observation on the new experience. For instance, an individual could learn just by observing or watching. This is how I have acquired my skills in painting or jewelry making. As I mentioned, I got a better understanding with all the mistakes and flaws that I had before. This modeling learning behavior would have a profound application of expanding company's culture. This is the reason that a leader should be the model on his members to improve the accomplishment of organization and individual objective.

Fostering a learning culture

In order to remain competitive and not left behind in today's modern world of business, a learning culture is necessary to promote in an organization. As a leader, he should demonstrate

a powerful leadership to the members by motivating them the capability to innovate and challenge status quo. First and foremost, a leader should develop a clear vision and knowledge on how it would be accomplished consistently. In this way, your members as you work together will see your capacity of being an effective leader that will help to improve its performance of an individual and an organization as an entire system. Keep in mind that employees that are more inspired and committed on their work are the ones that you would like to be your members and who could be a leader in the future. Nevertheless, it is only vital to maintain and guide them to appreciate their jobs and their achievements by acknowledging a learning behavior for individual, groups and the entire organization.

It is true that the role of a leader is to develop the atmosphere in an organization where his members or his teams learn and would have a subjective character the pattern of constant education. Moreover, it is a fact that effective communication between the leader and its member is essential in supporting the shared effort in learning organization. The leader should guide the progress of collaboration, transform, and increase the abilities of the team to work with the future of an organization. Therefore, it is only necessary that a leader has right knowledge in organizational change in order to sustain the present business environment and skills needed in managing a learning organization.

Lussier and Achua, Leadership: Theory, Application, & Skill Development, 5th ed., Boston, Cengage Learning, 2013.

E-COMMERCE MANAGEMENT

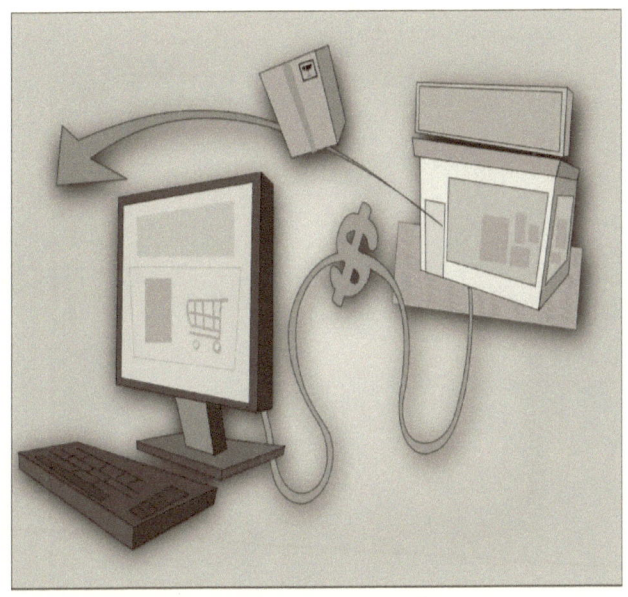

Compare the advantages of online job markets over traditional job markets on five characteristics.

Effective hiring process of any organization is one of the important factors that will help to accomplish and operate a successful business. However, finding a right person on the job is not easy tasks for a company. In the old days, to apply for a job is a traditional way where you can check the newspapers for a vacant position and sent an application by mail. I remembered that I was doing sending lots of application letters with a resume on many companies many years ago. At present, a rising technology has occurred in the method of recruiting an employee. The world of internet has brought to an advance element to many of the organization recruitment process. This approach has been a test to the traditional method of various factors of recruiting a prospective employee. In this essay, I will discuss the comparison of the advantages of online job markets over traditional job markets. These are based on the following five characteristics:

1. Cost
2. Applicant's comfort to find a job
3. Employer's capacity to search an applicant
4. Communication process
5. Place

Cost-effective is the first advantage of online job markets. It is true that the world of recruitment online is the best reasonable and suitable method compared with a traditional way which has step by step subsequent processes that incur expensive costs of hiring. An employer and a job agency could save a huge recruitment cost for which you do not have to spend thousands of dollars for various ways to advertise a job position such as printing or advertising costs. On the web, they can assist the progress of the application for variety of possibilities accessible to a firm. Although, it would need some enabled software applications and tools to accomplish this approach, it is still cost-saving from many areas of recruiting process of an organization.

In online job markets, an applicant has a comfort and ease to find a job. You have the opportunity in choosing a job you want to apply. Normally, you have to complete an application form and send it electronically; upload a resume or a cover letter. You have the chance to review it and to correct any mistakes before you finally submit it. A response will also be quicker from an employer since you will receive an email confirming of your application. Unlike in traditional, you will wait longer when you will receive a reply or receipt of confirmation. For instance, I had to send follow-up letters by mail on the applications that I have applied to some companies because I did not receive any responses. Nowadays, it is extremely an advantage to the applicants because they can able to access any types of jobs online. A job-seeker can also update or to edit a resume that has been uploaded in any job sites such as indeed.com or monster.com. In addition, they are many store companies that have their own touch-screen booth for individual who wants to search and apply for a job like Wal-Mart or Sears in which it is not available in a traditional approach.

Another advantage is that an employer is able to find an employee. Particularly, it is very useful if a company with a website where it will attract more applicants. In this way, it will be quicker and faster to connect with top candidates. With social networking like linkedin or facebook, an employer will be able to find the best candidate for the job of a lesser time of recruiting process where they could streamline the candidates qualified for the position. Further, an employer could able to review and perform background check on the candidate before actually setting an interview. It is certainly a time saving process of final hiring decision. Compared to traditional employment, you will get hundreds of hard copies of a resume being reviewed and assessed which would take you much of your time before you can actually interview them in person.

As the years passed by, the growth of the job markets online employee has opened an advance approach to faster communication process. In this case, the relationship between an employer and a potential employee becomes viable. The employer has the ability to send their message through emails to those shortlisted applicants especially when scheduled for interview. Regardless of the result of an interview, an applicant is also able to send a message or ask questions by email on the employer. The communication speed benefits largely both on an employer or a job-seeker. In traditional, it will delay any kind of response from and after the interview or status of an application. Likewise, companies have the ability to do video interviewing or taking a test online. In this case, an employer could be able to pre-screen, review, assess or sort out their prospective candidates easier. This process is something impossible to do in traditional job employment as there are various steps that will take place on recruitment process of a face to face basis.

And finally, the convenience of place to apply is one of the advantages of an online job market. Presently, an applicant has a chance to find a job of any location. The process is easy and faster since employers have the tools simplified and enhanced in hiring an employee, even out of town or out of a country. For instance, United Nations in Switzerland has a global portal online that you could able to search and apply a job position that matches your skills no matter where you are. The process would be convenient on a job-seeker and an employer with less time and cost. Any job vacancy posted online could be accessible to a larger audience locally and globally. This could be done by means of job agencies or websites, company websites or any social networks in which it has opportunity to find the best candidate. Even locally, this is not an easy process of a traditional way to accomplish a better result from hiring an employee. Moreover, it will cost more to advertise jobs globally.

To look for a good job and to search for a candidate perfect for the job could cost you a substantial amount of time and money and it can also be discouraging. Fortunately, online job market has tremendously developed on the way job-seekers hunting for a job or an employer finding a potential employee. As a result, many organizations save a lot of time for hiring process and costs as compared to traditional job market. Likewise, it can enhance the efficiency and success of the hiring process of any organization.

Turban, <u>*Electronic Commerce: A Managerial Perspective*</u>*, 6th ed., New Jersey, 2010.*

Evaluate the importance of customer loyalty and identify ways to increase e-loyalty.

In any company, customers are the essence of a successful business. It is only necessary to accommodate their needs and contentment of dealings with them. In a similar matter, customers reciprocate this positive experience in giving their loyalty to them. While gaining new shoppers is imperative in a business, keeping the current ones should be given a more attention. This is one of the reasons why a selling company goes down because they give lesser significance of customer loyalty. As a customer, I will show my loyalty if I have a desirable buying experience and treated me as a greater priority to their business. In this paper, I would like to discuss and analyze the importance of customer loyalty and its techniques on how to build it on the following paragraphs.

The growth of customer loyalty can lead to reduce cost measure of a business. It is true that it cost more to attract and gain new customer than to serve the current ones. It means that when a company trying to attract new customers, the company would spend a lot of money to advertise and educate them about their products and give them a complete service which a company could spend even more. By building loyalty to your current customer, it could influence other consumers to try your products in which it will reduce marketing and advertising costs of gaining new ones. Even if a seller or any selling company made some mistakes, a loyal customer is more forgiving and trusts them to resolve it. Vice versa, if a loyal customer complaint openly, a company would do the best effort to solve the problem. For instance, I am a loyal buyer at Ebay. On my last transaction, I had encountered problem with the seller so I had to complain it at Ebay. I was satisfied the way they handled and resolved the issue and even more committed to continue buying products of them.

Another importance of customer loyalty is it also enhances the state of a market of a company. This means that if a company would like to introduce a new product or brand, the customer will likely willing to give it a try. A company that puts their best effort to relate and improve loyalty to their customers would result from not switching to the competitor. In time of cost inflation, the customer's commitment to stand up to your product or brand will help to assure of not luring them away and turn down competition. Moreover, customer loyalty can lessen in price sensitivity. What does it mean? The relationship of a seller to the customers that drive the loyalty to them is not because of a product's low price. Price is not as important to the customer as they acknowledge the value that a seller provides which could arise out of good customer service, convenience or aspect of a product. In this case, it is only worth to maintain and offer good value and relationship to the customers.

Gaining agreeable word-of- mouth referral or feedback is one of the most effective marketing strategy when it comes building your brand. Loyal customers are free marketing ambassadors of your product. They can give good recommendations and share their affirmative experience in the product of other consumers. For example, I always encourage other consumer to try a product that I normally used by writing a product review. Sometimes, I answer questions or concerns about the product asked by a prospective buyer which usually comes at Amazon.

Customers are significant in achieving a successful business. So it is only essential to give them a full satisfaction from their purchasing experience in which it would be easier technique to develop e-loyalty. The three most common ways to increase it is: learn the needs of the customers, interaction with customers, and provide excellent customer service.

- **Learn the needs of the customers.** It is significant in any business to expect what the customer wants. It is not only enough to persuade them to buy your products. Hence, it is vital to understand and recognize what really the customer needs which is normally based on their lifestyle and preference. Once you get that information, you can use it to convince them that purchasing your product is in their optimum interest.

- **Interaction with customers.** It is good to maintain connection with the customers by communicating even after the sales. In this case, you are building ongoing association with them by asking them a feedback on their purchase experience or how you can make them serve better. For this reason, it helps a customer's impression that their business is important and acknowledges their satisfaction on what a company can more offer to them. Interaction with customer is normally done by sending them a newsletter, blogs or through social media.

- **Provide excellent customer service.** I believe that this is all what customer wants in their purchase journey. Simple website, ease to find products or not complicated checkout process are things that a customer expects in order to come back and make their life simple. As a customer, for instance, I do not like when I started to shop online and then at the checkout process, shipping cost is not included until on payment process. Sometimes, the product is out of stock or back order. Most of the times when this happens, I would just emptied my cart and do not come back. Why could they just let the shopper know at hand that the product is out of stock? Also, I would prefer when they have online chat service. In this case, it would not only that a customer could directly ask questions or inquiry but also it could create a relationship to them. This is a great opportunity for a seller or a company to learn what a customer really needs.

As a summary, it is true that gaining new customer is a difficult part of a business but how to keep them back is another story. However, if a company or a seller knows how to build customer loyalty, it would be for a long-term advantage on the business. As a result, loyal customer could have more sales transactions, refer more consumers and more agreeable to extend their buying journey into unique categories.

Turban, <u>Electronic Commerce: A Managerial Perspective</u>, 6th ed., New Jersey, 2010.

Briefly describe Web 2.0. How does it differ from the traditional Web?

Since the internet has been developed, the rising technology plays a significant aspect in the progress of giving and exchanging information. The evolution of the technology was changed differently from the traditional Web in which the user could only avail to navigate the web pages to that current web technology referred to Web 2.0. This changing trend of using the internet enhances the website by a large range collection of data technologies and web applications including blogs, wikis, social bookmarking and RSS. In Web 2.0, the users have the opportunity to participate in the progress and expansion of the web by collaborating and connected with other web users socially instead of just viewing its web content. The primary goal of Web 2.0 is aimed to improve the comprehension on sharing and ability to maintain more connection than the traditional way of communicating such as email.

Some of the general characteristics of Web 2.0 are as follows:

1. The web pages usually mixed in its content of single or multiple sources.
2. The ease of access and use of application through internet.
3. The user develops any type of information on the web in an online community or simply called "user-generated content".
4. The user contributes and takes part in the content of the web according to their preference
5. It is about social networking and computing.

6. It uses the connection as a platform in which user is able to access software applications online.

As we examine to the beginning of the internet, Web 2.0 describes by higher collaboration and user communication that improves connection channels. Traditional Web and Web 2.0 have several factors which is different from each other. In order to be more precise to the subject matter, I would like to discuss it further in the following paragraphs.

Web 2.0 is a two-way communication. It means that the user has an opportunity to exchange ideas or views to another user and vice versa. It can also be in various way to connect and response in a group. For instance, Facebook and Twitter are examples of website that users interact to each others. This connection between the users makes it considerably different. On the contrary, traditional Web is one-way communication. It has no interaction involved in the users because the connection is only between the web administrator or owner and the client or user. Let us put this way. Web 2.0 is a dialogue where you listen to a person and responded it back while traditional Web is like a book or an instruction that you only read and learn from it.

In terms of content of information, the users in Web 2.0 take part in sharing and maintaining its content. The information is active and current. For example, Wikipedia updates the information as it changes the current data onto specific individual or things frequently. Each user has the chance to contribute and add information on its content. Users participate in blogging and tagging activity which is normally used for a guide or search. On the other hand, traditional Web is created for the purpose of reading or viewing only which is only provided by the owner of the website. In this matter, the users have no opinion into the nature and aspect of its content. The web pages have fixed information and only updated once in a while. Each link between the website could only open a page to read or to download. In fact, it prevents them from doing the blogging and the tagging in which the users enjoy in the Web 2.0.

Another significant difference is regarding web designing. In web 2.0, the web pages are more creative in structure by getting the users to be involved and taking part of the static web information of traditional Web. Useful technological aid from them can be an additional growth of prospective layout of data of the web. They can create a design or templates with the use of basic website tools available in order to have a more attractive homepages. In this case, it will bring them an agreeable and exciting browsing journey. Unlike in traditional, the expert on the web or an individual that has knowledge of web creation is the only ones who can control and execute the designs of the website. As a web user, I would only have passive and less interesting browsing activity in traditional Web.

In conclusion, I could see how the development of the internet has progressed. Web 2.0 has associated with the growth of the Web-based virtual online community and internet services which considers having a great development particularly within the course of business transaction. As a result, it has a better working relation to clients or customers, associate, merchants and internet users. However, the differences between these two technologies make it particularly important to each user online in their own way. It only depends on what they intend to do in their search. Web 2.0 and traditional Web have its own purpose of reaching their users.

Turban, Electronic Commerce: A Managerial Perspective, 6th ed., New Jersey, 2010.

Analyze the similarities and differences between laws and ethics.

Law and ethics are two of the significant element connected in every individual's behavior that has effect on each daily lives. So what could be the consequences that do not conform to ethical and legal system either in business practices and the professionals? Since these two elements have similarities on the way to penalize or to discourage any wrong doing, they are completely different from its aspect and how it functions. We might recognize some individual conduct as wrong but not such behavior is against the law or a behavior to be good for some but unethical to others. For this reason, law and ethics is inevitably a different thing. In this essay, I will discuss further how they can be similar and different to each other.

First, let us start what does law and ethics mean. Law is a set of rules and regulations enacted by a higher authority to provide guidance for human behavior. On the other hand, ethics is set of codes based on moral standards. Many of us puzzled that law and ethic are same concept but they are actually distinct from each other. Nevertheless, they have some similar characteristics. For example, they are both written rules which apply to all individuals or particular groups on a daily basis. Both of these will help to keep up for its moral boundary and to prevent from breaking of those rules. This tells us how we shall behave in a certain situation. The law can oblige the people to follow for what they think to be unethical behavior. For instance, professionals like a doctor, lawyer or teacher have code of ethics. They are doing the jobs within the legal aspect of their profession and ethics has the big part in performing their duties accordingly. Therefore, if failed to obey it, you could be ethically accountable and charge with such wrongdoing. Another example is drunk driving. Driving under the influence of alcohol is not only unethical but it is against the law. Law and ethics have impact to each other profoundly. It must reflect the accepted moral beliefs of a society in order to be effective. Sometimes law acts to initiate its good character and maintain this condition as it may influence the growth of ethics.

Laws and ethics are attained almost entirely sphere of the people. As I talked about their similarities previously, they have also distinguishing aspect in certain manners. Some question could help us to determine the distinction such as "What would be the punishment if you break a rule?" Let us cite some instances. The operation of a business is all administered by law. In case a company violates one of these rules, he is accountable to such violation and will be legally punish. In some cases, the consequences could pay fines, imprisonment or shutting down a business. On the other hand, the ethical negligence would not normally involve a punishment. Yet, the implication might result some conflict, hostility or problem. For example, an employee coming to work late or showing laziness in his duty might be written up or he might be suspended.

Further, they are key characteristics of law that makes it different from ethics. Law is consistent and firm in which there is no conflict to its requirement for the society to obey it. It means that it is precisely affirmed what is lawful or unlawful. This requirement is declared in written forms to be enforced, generally accepted by the people. It must be appropriate in general on the same character in a similar set of situations in any given place. Any breach of law will lead to some punishment as I mentioned in the previous paragraph. Robbery, for instance, is a criminal act that you will be prosecuted if found guilty.

On the contrary, ethics is variable. It means that the right and wrong choice of actions change from \the basis of certain situations. Ethics does not oblige to be published neither enforced to be obeyed to the society. For a reason, it depends on a person to person grounds or matter of choice in associating with other groups or people from any location. If you do not follow the rules of ethics, you may not be punished though as I stated before, you would face consequences of your behavior. In the business, for example, it is ethical to greet or shake the hands of your business partner or customer. If you failed to do that, you are not to be penalized. However, this behavior might be resulted in a bad reputation for the business or other party might feel that they are not welcome.

In summary, both law and ethics works together in order to maintain the conduct and strength of the society. Although their similarities and differences is a very complex subject, they are definitely highly essential in the daily activities to be followed whether it is business organization, professionals, or in public interests. They are binding together to determine on which how the people or group decided to communicate or collaborate with each and every member of the society.

Turban, Electronic Commerce: A Managerial Perspective, 6th ed., New Jersey, 2010.

THE RESEARCH PROCESS

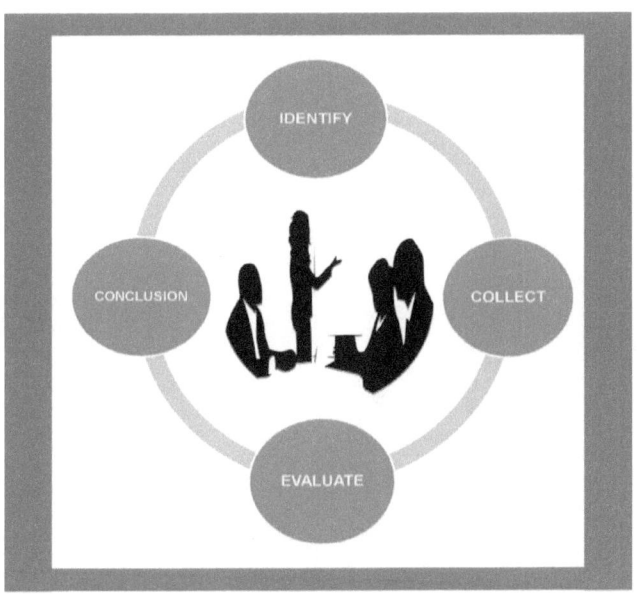

Discuss the different types of sources (i.e. general, primary, and secondary). What are the differences among these sources? Why is it important that researchers utilize primary sources when conducting a thorough review of the literature?

To prepare a literature review, the writer acquires collection of facts and information from the various sources to compile and construct an argument regarding the subject. It needs only to recognize what sources can be used in a research. In this essay, I will discuss about the subject: its types, their differences and the more important type to use in writing a literature review.

There are vast of sources available to choose from in conducting a literature review. These sources are classified as follows:

General Source

This type consists of compilation of information on the primary and secondary sources. The information on general sources considers two matters: it provides to use as a start to collect general knowledge to a new subject and provides some ideas where to gather relevant and helpful sources on a specific subject. General sources can be useful for a study of research. However, it is not advisable to use it in a research to support an argument. It is normally made to simple and does not have recent information. As a result, many of the experts are skeptical on using them.

The most commonly used of general sources are dictionaries, encyclopedia, handbook, manuals, database, book reviews, and other related sources.

Primary Sources

The information on this category is a firsthand writing of the author. That is to say, the information was first originated in this source. It is usually written on an actual period of an event with all the facts related to the subject including the examination, outcome of an argument and other data associated on the event. For example, a doctor achieved a discovery about a medicine to cure a certain illness. An article or journal that he wrote about this research is a primary source. It is the most significant and useful information that serves as the utmost direct connection between the researchers and individual self-interest. Other primary examples are abstract collections, letters, diaries, interviews, government or legal documents and other first hand writings. It can also be non-written such as pictures, paintings, movies, drawing and other original art works.

Secondary Sources

The information on this category is written afterwards an event or experience has happened. It is typically that secondary sources examine, criticize or give remarks or opinions on the original work of other writers. Journals, articles, abstract or art works are primary sources. Nevertheless, these can also be secondary sources if an author is evaluating, examine or revising its primary source. For instance, let us take the previous example of a doctor's journal on his new medicine discovery. It would be a secondary source, if an author of an article has written his observations and analysis on the said journal. Other secondary sources are textbooks, reference books, bibliographies, newspapers, commentaries, and other related printed materials.

One of the concerns of a researcher conducts a literature review is to know what would be the difference in these types of sources. Thus, recognizing its difference is the best approach to conform the requirements of a research paper. The following are the things that differ from these types of sources.

General Sources	Primary Sources	Secondary Sources
1. It is a combination of information on primary and secondary sources.	It contains raw evidence, and firsthand document.	It contains no direct evidence and secondhand document.
2. It is normally written on a later period.	It is written on actual direct observation.	It is written after an event has happened.
3. The author is a non-participant of an event.	The author is a participant or a witness for a study.	The author is a non-participant of an event
4. The information is precise and a plain repackage of facts.	The information is recent and broader.	It is easier to understand the information included.

In conducting a literature review, it is essential for a researcher to acknowledge where to acquire information on a specific study. It is true that you can begin your research through the use of secondary sources but it is agreeable to gather further information on the primary sources. There are reasons why researchers prefer to use primary sources. For instance, I know that I can make a better paper using it based on my sole assessment and examination in the field of a subject. Thus, I can learn and develop a more logical and analytical way of thinking as I look closely and carefully examines facts and evidence on primary sources. The query about primary sources strengthens to argue and analyze with comparison of various sources that serve contradicting opinions. Hence, it can develop a profound and broader comprehension on how these sources have been created. Once the paper has finished, you know that you just did not read it but you carefully analyze and explain in your own understanding relating an experience reading these materials.

In conclusion, using all types of sources can be useful and beneficial to complete a literature review. Although, primary sources are the most important sources to conduct a research, I believe that a combination of different sources can create a more significant result and a well-written review of the literature.

Salkind, <u>Exploring Research</u>, 8th ed., New Jersey, 2012.

Outline the four steps in the data collection process. Explain why it is so important to be systematic in collecting data.

In any type of fields of a subject, you collect appropriate information to examine a hypothesis or support an answer to a research query. This means that it has to be arranged and gathered in a systematic way for agreeable meaning and satisfactory outcomes. According to Neil Salkind, it contains four steps in the process of data collection. These are: construct a data collection form, establish a coding strategy, gathering of actual information, and data collection entry.

The first step is to construct a data collection form. This is important step that can be used to record points and ease of analysis application on the information gathered. The data collection form should be characterized as stated in the 4th commandment of collection of data. It means that a participant on the activity should understand the procedure correctly and the clarity of answering the questions. In order to test your material and your questionnaires, it should be practice with an individual or two to determine that it all works well. In this case, if there is a problem or errors, it will allow you to change it in order to make a more agreeable to them. To diminish an error, it is advantageous to use a spreadsheet for the information on the first sheet because it tallies what is on the screen which it will give you an easier job. The information relevant to the questions is collected and inserted into the columns and rows on the basis of current variables. Each form should be dated with initials. To avoid damage or loss, keep at least two copies of a different storage as stated in 5th commandment of data collection.

The second step is to establish a coding strategy. This will help to save time and aid the progress of examining the data and effective recording. A coding format is available for an easy analysis. There are various ways how coding can be done, it could be a number, symbol or letter. It only depends on what types of information to be coded or which fits to its classification. It is important to emphasize that making the coding system simpler will be better. For instance as cited in the textbook, you are coding for a gender of the child. You can use 1 to represent a male and 2 for a female. Thus, the coding should be clear, accurate and understandable as mentioned in the previous paragraph.

To gather actual information on data collection is the third step. This is where you should adhere the 7th commandment of data collection. This means that you have to determine beforehand what types of information to be needed and where it will be accumulated. Collecting data is taking up a great deal of time so creating a detailed planning for all essential aspects of the analysis is necessary which provides the accomplishments of this process of a complete and timely way. The use of optical scanner which reads the responses from the questionnaires and matches it with a key is a useful scoring option. The cost of this machine might be costly but it will be very beneficial to the time and money spent on it. As the technology growing fast, there are also smartphones with an operating system which is a newest technology that is developing rapidly to set up and build according to specifications.

The final step is an entry of information on the data collection form. This is where the original data will be coded onto the form where it can be easily analyzed and checked accordingly. Regardless of how you consider scoring the results, it is significant that you be able to see at a coded sheet in which you will have a chance to compile and arrange what is actually occurring in your data and confirm the validity of the information. It is good that somebody can help out to perform this process. However, it is significant to remember the 6th commandment of data collection. It means that you have to be confident that an individual is knowledgeable in the process. It should also keep in mind the 5th commandment as mentioned in the previous paragraph. Further, never get rid off the original information as stated in the 10th commandment of data collection. You might still need those in the future reference.

Regardless of what classification is your data collection, it is vital in the principle of research to ensure that it is in order and correct. Can you analyze or test information that is not organized? If this is the case, it will not give you an easy analysis on the data gathered. Further, it will be hard to detect any possible errors or problem in an effort for a research. Usually, errors made because an individual is considerably influenced by whatever sources of information accessible and do not realize that the impact on this information might not really show any evidence to test or support the hypothesis. For this reason, a systematic data collection will give clear evidence and an easier interpretation of achieving a purpose of your analysis.

Data collection is the essence to determine the value of research regarding any field of interest where the subsequent conclusion to be made is based on the validity of your findings. Therefore, it is very significant to follow steps in collecting data in which can be performed systematically in reaching the result.

Salkind, <u>Exploring Research</u>, 8th ed., New Jersey, 2012.

Distinguish qualitative research methods from those categorized as quantitative methods. Outline what types of questions qualitative research addresses that cannot be addressed by quantitative research.

In performing a research, you need to gather information on various sources of information about a specific study in order to achieve a systematic and reasonable argument. There are two types of research method that can be applied for performing this task. These are: qualitative and quantitative approach. These two approaches differ from each other and have their own advantage that grants you the best possible examination on every topic of interest and formulate a conclusion of an adequate way. I would like to discuss factors of the distinction of these research methods of the following paragraphs.

The basic objective of a qualitative research is to bring the comprehensive and accurate information of a specific study. This means that a researcher is concern in sustaining a deeper and richer comprehension and interpretation of an individual motivation and behavior on a certain concept. This approach is generally subjective on a study to be examined. In contrast, the focal point of concern in a quantitative research is to create and apply mathematical or statistical description or hypothesis of a specific event or occurrence. This approach leads to stay objectively in a manner that it looks for accurate measurement and examination of the course of a study in response of the research questions.

Regarding on how a data collected, these two research methods are also distinct from each other. Qualitative research collects information on the form of non-mathematical such as words, images and objects. Primary and secondary sources are where to gather valuable information in supporting an argument on a particular subject which can be obtained from a range of methods in collecting a data. These sources include narrative interviews where the researcher asks questions on an individual, observation either directly present or an active participant in the field of study or focus groups where a small group of people discussing their views and insight on a certain topic. Other related sources are documentation, archival records and artifacts. On the other hand, a data gathered in quantitative involving statistical examination are to enhance a data numerically that can be applied to test the relationship of variables. The information is collected by numerous ways in order to conform a concrete procedure and arrange for mathematical analysis. This examination provides an individual to find out to what degree is a connection with two or more variables. A data can be acquired from a larger group of people by asking a list of questions on a survey or questionnaires.

In most cases, research questions on qualitative are open-ended. This means that you would provide to reply a question on your own understanding and point of view on the concept. This makes it different from the quantitative because of the absence of numerical significance required for a precise research. For instance, in writing an essay, you have to explain and analyze your answer to the subject matter in which it asks the questions. Responding to this question would spend you a great deal of time. Unlike in quantitative, the questions are closed-ended such as what, when, where or how many. These are specific questions that you have an option to select an answer without giving an insight on the subject and comparatively simple and fast. When you are taking a product survey, for instance, it is normally with yes or no response to a question, or it can also be a multiple choice question.

In general, there are questions categorized in qualitative research which cannot be recognized in a quantitative approach. In order to be able to have a non-mathematical data to achieve a better result, it is better to know the following qualitative research methods.

- **Case studies.** This research pertains to a complete and precise data on the concept in connection to a study that is being examined. This is usually a particular means of acquiring information about the behavior of a person or group of individuals for a number of reasons. A researcher develops a research question, gathers its information on a variety of sources available either primary or secondary to support an argument and then examine it.

- **Ethnographies.** Originate from the word "ethno", it signifies race or culture. This can also be a case study. However, it involves specifically the analysis of customs and culture of an individual or organization from a particular society or place in which a researcher has an active part on the study. It means that he is sharing his experience and participating in the activity on day-to-day where the study is acquired.

- **Historical Research.** From the root word "history", it clearly indicates past events that have been examined. This often searches to find "how or why" things happened on the past and these events establish in connection to the current or in future times. Both primary and secondary sources provide significant information. Hence, it would be better to use primary sources of conducting this research if available because they have more detailed and accurate information at hand.

All these qualitative research methods explore comprehensive background information and its argument thoroughly in which the type of questions cannot be recognized in quantitative. For example, a researcher conducts a study to develop a new technology for surgical procedure. The analysis to be made in this study involves in-depth reasoning, encouragement for individual behavior or how they react on a certain situation and other related human interactions. The application of this new technology affects the achievement on a conclusion accomplished a theory of how combined knowledge within a group of individuals in which they have no mathematical sense to be applied for quantitative research. Further, the research questions are mostly open-ended such as "why" and "how". This type of questions cannot be applied for quantitative research.

In summary, I conclude that qualitative examines the data collected into a theory while quantitative examines the theory turned into a data. It is vital to acknowledge the distinction of applying to these two approaches in conducting a study. This knowledge can guide a researcher to select the suitable approach from a certain study to be performed properly.

Salkind, Exploring Research, 8th ed., New Jersey, 2012.

Outline the basic "rule of thumb" that researchers follow when formatting a manuscript for publication.

Someday, you may have a favorable circumstance to give a manuscript in consideration for publication. As much the content of your paper is remarkably important, the way how it is formatted will also take significance of achieving acceptance of a manuscript. As we know, there are some requirements to be followed on how to arrange a manuscript. The Publication of the American Psychology Association (6th ed., 2009) makes a lists of suggestion and guidelines on how a manuscript to be formatted according to their standard rule. There is a basic "rule of thumb" when formatting a manuscript for publication that helps to organize the process. It is a short guidelines which I am about to discuss in this essay.

1. **Type should be readable.** Bear in mind, it is important that your paper is easy to read and clear because it would gain you a good chance a manuscript acceptance. In addition, it will give a positive impact on your readers. To be readable, it is necessary to check a proper use of text, spacing, margin, alignment or indention which can be done by setting it up in Microsoft Word menu for proper formats.

2. **Text font and size.** It should be 12-point New Times Roman and caption for figure is Arial. Though it is not necessary to use this font, APA recommended this font because it has bigger and clearer strokes at the tip of the major parts of each letter which is easier to read. This is also better in your eyes when you are reading longer.

Remember, your goal is the readability of your manuscript. On the other hand, Sans Serif font like Arial is not advisable in using text in a manuscript. This font is only ideal in figure captions because it brings you an up-to-date and more streamlined appearance. By following this rule, it may create as much good outcome on how a manuscript is accepted just as it is in content.

3. **Spacing.** All lines should be double-spaced. This means that double spacing should take place on the entire manuscript including the headings, title or figure captions. I believed that this is for the purpose of reading and making notes on those blank lines by the editor.

4. **Margin.** All sides should have 1 inch margin. This is a standard margin on the top, bottom, left and right of each page which leave a space for the editor to make notes again. It will also aid to avoid your work from looking disorderly.

5. **Numbering of pages.** Every page should be numbered with Arabic numerals. To create a page number on every page, use the page number menu at Microsoft Word. The following are separate pages so each of them should be numbered separately. The title page which is the front page and the first thing you see in a manuscript should be numbered 1.

    a. The abstract which is a concise overview of a manuscript should be numbered 2.

    b. The text which is the main body of a manuscript should start with number 3.

   c. The rest of the parts of a manuscript such as references, footnotes and others are on different pages which are consecutively numbered. Nonetheless, any artwork or figures should not be numbered because it is segregated from a manuscript in a different file.

6. **Indention.** Each time you make a new paragraph, it should be indented at least 5 to 7

   spaces or half an inch. I normally do this when I copy and paste my essay since it won't indent automatically. However, you can set up automatic indention when you are working at Microsoft Word in paragraph option.

7. **Alignment.** The text should be aligned to the left for an easier reading. For example, when you are reading, your eyes moves on the same edge from left to right which leaves a "right ragged margin". This will also help an editor to discover if you have any problem with spacing on your manuscript.

8. **Headings.** The application of heading is useful to demonstrate to your readers on how your manuscript is arranged by describing the parts and by pointing out which those are evenly significant and less important to others. Heading in most documents which are lengthy and have subsections have three different levels which are used and typed as follows:

   a. First-level should be typed centered, upper and lower case.

Journal of a Joyful Season

The passion for writing is not just a talent or a gift. I am not really experienced or an expert on the subject but my keen interest in writing a poem will give me a reason to pursue it.

---

b. Second-level should be typed flush-left, upper and lower case.

Journal of a Joyful Season

The passion for writing is not just a talent or a gift. I am not really experienced or an expert on the subject but my keen interest in writing a poem will give me a reason to pursue it.

---

c. Third level should be typed boldface, indented, and lower case.

Journal of a joyful season. The passion for writing is not just a talent or a gift. I am not really experienced or an expert on the subject but my keen interest in writing a poem will give me a reason to pursue it.

---

9. **Punctuation Marks.** As a standard rule, it should leave one space after each punctuation mark except on some cases, for instance abbreviating a phrase, name or country as in United States for U.S.

10. **Abstract.** You should not indent an abstract because it does not contain a paragraph. As mentioned in guideline #2, it shows on a separate page and it should be numbered 2.

11. **References.** These are the lists of the sources that a writer had collected and examined from a research. This is shown at the end of your writing and started on a separate page.

In conclusion, formatting a manuscript is an important step in submission of publication. What is the use of a well-written content of an article if it is not properly formatted? The appearance of your paper gives a good impression of the eyes to the editor. In order to look your paper more professional, it has to follow guidelines to format a manuscript properly. For doing so, a researcher has a good chance of acceptance and it lessens the time for publication.

[1]*Salkind, Exploring Research, 8th ed., New Jersey, 2012.*
[2]*Publication Manual of the American Psychology Association, http://www.apastyle.org, 6th ed., Washington, 2009.*

REFERENCES

1. *Lepak, David, __Human Resource Management__, 1ˢᵗ Ed. New Jersey: Pearson, 2009.*

2. *Department of Labor, __Equal Employment Opportunity/Compliance__, www.dol.gov.*

3. *National Relation Labor Board, __Employee Rights__, http://www.nlrb.gov/rights-we-protect/employee-rights.*

4. *National Relation Labor Board, __NLRA__, www.nlrb.gov/national-labor-relations-act*

5. *Deresky, __International Management: Managing Across Borders and Cultures__, 5ʰ ed., New Jersey: Pearson, 2006*

6. *Cheeseman, __Contemporary Business and Online Commerce Law__, 6ᵗʰ Ed. New Jersey: Pearson, 2009.*

7. *Lectric Law Library, O.K. City Bombing Trial 2/96 Order Granting Change of Venue to Denver, __www.lectlaw.com__*

8. *Legal Information Institute, Uniform Commercial Code, __http://www.law,cornell.edu.__*

9. *Pinto, __Project Management: Achieving Competitive Advantage__, 2ⁿᵈ ed., New Jersey, 2010*

10. *David, __Strategic Management: Concept and Cases__, 12ᵗʰ ed., New Jersey, 2009.*

11. *Legal Information Institute, __U.S. Code: Title 11-Bankruptcy__, http://www.law.cornell.edu/uscode/text/11*

12. *Kotler, Keller, __Marketing Management__, 13ᵗʰ ed., New Jersey: Pearson, 2009*

13. *Company Profile, About Rubbermaid Commercial Products, LLC, http://www.rubbermaidcommercial.com/rcp/company/*

14. *Rob Wagner, Hyundai Car History, http://www.ehow.com/about 5243229 history-hyundai-cars.htm*

15. *George,Jones, Understanding and Managing: Organizational Behavior, 5^h ed., New Jersey: Pearson, 2008*

16. *DeGeorge, Business Ethics, 7th ed., New Jersey, Pearson/Prentice Hall, 2010.*

17. *Lussier and Achua, Leadership: Theory, Application, & Skill Development, 5th ed., Boston, Cengage Learning, 2013.*

18. *Turban, Electronic Commerce: A Managerial Perspective, 6th ed., New Jersey, 2010.*

19. *Salkind, Exploring Research, 8th ed., New Jersey, 2012.*

20. *Publication Manual of the American Psychology Association, http://www.apastyle.org, 6th ed., Washington, 2009.*

"For the Lord gives wisdom; from his mouth come knowledge and understanding."

Proverbs 2:6

www.ingramcontent.com/pod-product-compliance
Lightning Source LLC
Chambersburg PA
CBHW020314290526
45785CB00007B/2796